P9-CQH-942

"*In Marriage: A Spiritual Journey*, Kathy Heskin draws on the experience of her own life to offer fresh perspective on the enduring mystery of married love. She writes with clarity, candor, and charm, and illuminates the Christian tradition as a vital resource for couples on this shared journey of faith."

Evelyn and James Whitehead
Authors of *Wisdom of the Body: Making Sense of our Sexuality*

"Kathy Heskin writes in a very readable style that avoids being preachy, maudlin, or pious. Her insights, both humorous and profound, are as pertinent to married couples seeking to enrich their marriage as they are to those who serve in marriage preparation and marriage enrichment ministry."

Paul Covino
Liturgist and editor,
Celebrating Marriage: Preparing the Wedding Liturgy

"This is a sophisticated, contemporary theological reflection of a Christian, Catholic woman on her experience of marriage."

John Shea
Theologian and author,
Gospel Light: Jesus Stories for Spiritual Consciousness

"What a delightful book on marriage! It is full of practical steps to making a marriage the best it can be. This book that can give inspiration and practical help to all married couples, no matter what season of their marriage they are in."

Lee & Jan Kremer
Worldwide Marriage Encounter

"Kathy's story will call each of us to a deeper engagement with the life and love, celebration and suffering, death and rebirth at the heart of our relationships."

Paul Giblin, Ph.D.
Loyola University Chicago Institute of Pastoral Studies

Marriage
a Spiritual Journey

Kathy Heskin

TWENTY-THIRD PUBLICATIONS
185 Willow Street • PO BOX 180 • MYSTIC, CT 06355
TEL: 1-800-321-0411 • FAX: 1-800-572-0788
E-MAIL: ttpubs@aol.com • www.twentythirdpublications.com

Bayard

Dedication

To my husband, Neil
who helped me find God in places I didn't expect,
and in the unexpected events of our life together.
Thank you.

The Scripture passages contained herein are from the *New Revised Standard Version of the Bible,* copyright ©1989, by the Division of Christian Education of the National Council of Churches of Christ in the U.S.A. All rights reserved.

Twenty-Third Publications
A Division of Bayard
185 Willow Street
P.O. Box 180
Mystic, CT 06355
(860) 536-2611
(800) 321-0411
www.twentythirdpublications.com

© Copyright 2002 Kathy Heskin. All rights reserved. No part of this publication may be reproduced in any manner without prior written permission of the publisher. Write to the Permissions Editor.

ISBN:1-58595-185-4
Library of Congress Catalog Card Number: 2001135548
Printed in the U.S.A.

Contents

Introduction

Last year I was asked to speak to the Young Adult Ministries Conference on the topic of the Catholic church's teaching on sexuality and marriage. I love to work with young adults, and find that they are anxious to know more about relationships and about living holy lives, so I looked forward to the conference. I had a pretty good talk planned, but no opening line. In the car on the way to the conference, I prayed for a hook to begin my talk. I immediately noticed that the car next to mine had a bumper sticker that read, "My Karma Has Overwhelmed My Dogma." A quick prayer of thanks and I was set. When I shared the moment with the people in my room, they laughed. I pointed out that the line was funny, but it also said something very important about the woman whose car sported the bumper sticker. Whenever she had an important decision to make, she probably only consulted one source, her own experience. And one source is not enough!

In the work I do with people studying ministry, one fundamental piece of the education process is Theological Reflection. To do this it is important to consult more than one source, to hold a conversation between lived experience, the tradition of the church—often the Scriptures—and the culture in which we find ourselves. This conversation, this bringing together the important things that form us, teaches a great deal. My husband Neil and I have used this kind of reflection in many ways in our lives. We often take a story from Scripture, the Sunday gospel, or a parable or miracle of Jesus, and try to connect our story to *the* story. When we do this we are transformed.

In this book I will try to make some of these connections for the reader. We have been blessed with faith and have tried to live our lives in the context of that faith. At times we have done this well, at other times we have failed miserably. I have tried not to slant my story too much in either direction, because all of us are a combination of both.

You will learn from my story that I am not terribly concerned with details. When I sent my draft of *Marriage: A Spiritual Journey*, to friends for suggestions, every one of them asked me who my audience was. For whom did I write this book? As I thought about it (for the first time) I realized one answer was "For me." Putting down my reflections on paper has always been a very important discipline and spiritual tool for me. I have learned a great deal from writing this. Because I feel reflection is vital to growth and because it helped me so much, I have included questions at the end of each chapter, which you may find useful. It is possible that people in committed relationships may learn something about each other if they share their answers with each other.

Another answer would be that I wrote it for Neil, my husband. We have had an incredible thirty-four year journey, filled with times of great happiness and times of terrible hurt. His patience and trust in me have caused me to grow into myself, to forgive my past hurts, and to become more of a lover. I have learned to be wife from Neil, and he has learned to be husband from me. All that I understand about relationship, I have learned with Neil. We are still in the process of learning, and I am very grateful for everything he has been and done for me. This book is written to thank him. I know that in some places you might want to hear his side or his story. You'll have to ask him to tell you; I can only tell my own story.

Besides the two of us, this book might be interesting to people who work with engaged and married couples, or to the engaged couples themselves. Young married couples may read and avoid some of our pitfalls. "Seasoned" couples might find a vehicle to retrace their steps and bless certain parts of their lives. I hope that others, in reading our story, may find a connection between their lives and the Scriptures. I especially have in mind those couples whom you see in restaurants, not talking to each other; or the husband or wife who sits in a parking lot at night because they have had a fight with their spouse and have nowhere to go; or those people who have lost themselves in work, or television, or the internet. Neil and I have been in some of these places, and they are hard places to be. One insight for all of us is that we have to tell each other our stories honestly, and listen with love.

When I think of people I wish to thank for helping with this book, I am deeply grateful to Neil for being my first reader, for letting me use our stories, and more importantly for helping me to live them. I am grateful to our children, Pete, Tom, and Paul, for teaching me how to be their mother; and to Tom's wife, Heather, for showing me how to be her mother-in-law. Each of these family members has taught me so much about myself and about how to love. They are people of great promise, and it is a joy to watch them as they grow into owning their life stories. Each one brings a different gift to me, and I thank them. Our twin grandsons, Justen and Mason, will be my newest teachers in relationship. Born March 1, 2000, they have opened a new chapter in our lives.

Because of our ministry as mentors to engaged couples, I wish to thank all of the couples who have come to Neil and me as they prepare for their marriages. They look to us for wisdom, but they bring a freshness and optimism that has enriched our relationship over the years. Each retreat or evening of romance for married couples that Neil and I have given has also been an opportunity to learn more about our own relationship. This has all been gift.

I am indebted to the friends who have read and edited, corrected and encouraged my writing. I want to thank Neil, Jim and Evelyn Whitehead, Roger and Cara Keller, Colette Wisnewski, Carole Colantoni, Jack Shea, Rosemary Carroll, and Peter Gilmour for all that they brought to this project. I am grateful for Maureen Harrington's enthusiasm, which helped me start writing again when I was stuck. I am also thankful that Mary Stimming kept after me, and gave me so much help with questions for the chapters. Also included in this debt of thanks is my friend and mentor, John Buscemi. Whenever I struggle with an idea, he points me in the right direction. That gift was especially important as I wrote this book.

And finally I am grateful to Fr. Pat Brennan, who, when we went to him for marriage counseling during our second crisis in marriage, believed in us and helped us to find a way to love again. After several sessions he sent us to a Marriage Encounter weekend, and that made all the difference!

Prelude

You're not the kind that cries at weddings, are you?

Odd question from my good friend, as I told him about my weekend. "I not only cry at weddings, I cry when I'm in my car and an unknown wedding party drives by honking." I had just witnessed a very special wedding, the first of our children's friends to marry. Ever since our son Pete was nine, he and his friends James and Andy did everything together. All that changed when James met Jen, and now James and Jen are husband and wife.

It is hard to witness any wedding and remain unmoved, but this was a four-hankie one. Love has the ability to transform, and the joy and excitement of a wedding day is almost irresistible. So I cry for the pleasure of love and the pain of alienation which will surely occur at times in their life together. I cry in wonder at the power of reconciliation possible in any marriage, and at the privilege of creating a home together, of becoming parents together, and of growing old with a friend to share the journey. And I cry because they may lose jobs, will suffer hurts, will bury each other's parents—and possibly a child—and, at some time, perhaps accompany the other in a final illness. But, as I told my friend, my real reason for crying is the awe I feel for the promise of companionship through all of these joys and trials, and for the promise of support

5

through the growth and mystery that a lifetime holds.

Whether or not they know it, a newly married couple presents to us, the church, an invitation to participate in their love, their passion, their ability to give life and to reconcile, their willingness to mutually commit to the work of a lifetime together, as we try to live as a faith community. On their wedding day they ask us to journey with them as they learn to image God's love. And they ask us to share our own journey with them. This invitation, and our response, lies at the heart of the covenant within the Christian community.

Thirty-four years ago, Neil and I were the groom and bride, listening to this exhortation from the old rite of Catholic marriage.

This union then is most serious, because it will bind you together for life in a relationship so close and so intimate that it will profoundly influence your whole future. That future, with its hopes and disappointments, its successes and its failures, its pleasures and its pain, its joys and its sorrows, is hidden from your eyes.

This is the mystery into which each married couple enters. This is the "Yes," said without a manual, without a map, that begins their journey into the paschal mystery of Jesus, the dying and rising lived out in the new family formed that day.

Yes, I do cry at weddings.

ONE

Finding Abundance in Marriage

The Gift That Keeps on Giving

On the third day there was a wedding in Cana of Galilee, and the mother of Jesus was there. Jesus and his disciples had also been invited to the wedding. When the wine gave out, the mother of Jesus said to him, "They have no wine." And Jesus said to her, "Woman, what concern is that to you and to me? My hour has not yet come." His mother said to the servants, "Do whatever he tells you."

—John 2:1–11

Why would Jesus perform his first miracle at a wedding? It seems odd at first glance, especially since John is the only evangelist who tells us this story. Matthew, Mark, and Luke all begin with miracles in synagogues. In the movie *Soul Food*, the boy Ahmad begins the story of his family with his Aunt Bird's wedding because, as he says, "Everything happens at a wedding!" John must have agreed with this logic because he tells us, "On the third day there was a wedding in Cana of Galilee." All of us have been to weddings and anniversaries that make much of this first miracle recorded by John. Somehow this miracle is seen to bring dignity to marriage, or even to motherhood. After all, Jesus did what his mother asked him to do.

I think the story has less to do with weddings and mothers than it does with wine and love. Wine will forever symbolize the joy of being loved by God. That love is overflowing, and it fills six water jars, each holding twenty or thirty gallons. More than everyone in that small village could drink in a year. Abundant wine, meant to be tasted and shared.

Why a wedding? Because the love that is shared by a man and woman, making a commitment to one another for a lifetime, has the potential of filling six water jars, spilling over to family and friends, to those they meet throughout their lives. The bride and groom are the celebrants of their union, and they vow to live as a sign to the community that God is with us. Marriage is a symbol of possibility, and the couple who tries to live as that symbol makes God's love real in the world. Some of the fruits of this kind of marriage are unconditional love, a witness to real consensus, and hope for reconciliation. This is the abundance that a couple can share in their own relationship and that will spill over to their families, friends, and community, if the couple is willing to enter into mystery. These three qualities—unconditional love, consensus, and reconciliation—are at the core of a strong marriage.

A living sign

Through the sacramental nature of their relationship the married couple is a sign, whether or not they accept the call to live their marriage fully. In choosing to be a positive sign of God's love, couples are asked to love unconditionally and abundantly. This abundant love goes beyond scorekeeping, beyond expectations, and tries to affirm the other into life. Abundant love does not withhold affection until the underwear is picked up or every check is entered in the checkbook. It is difficult to let go of conditions like, "If you would just...." or "I'll love you when...," and simply love. But a couple whose life bears witness to this abundance gives us a glimpse of what God's love is like. That couple stands as a signpost pointing us to an unconditionally loving God.

Unconditional love

Neil has loved me unconditionally in my passion to study and go to school. As an eighteen-year-old woman I had no clue that a large part of my adult life would be spent in classes. In fact, after I met Neil I flunked out of college and went to secretarial school so that I would be able to get a good job and we could get married. Somewhere in the first few years of our life together, I decided that I wanted to finish college. And so I began to take a class or two every semester. Before we had children it was fairly easy, but once our boys were born, it was quite a trick to get sitters or to take them to the preschool at the college; to study and also to make the meals and do things like cleaning. I even gave birth during finals one year, which was a real interruption. And taking Cultural Anthropology while I was large with child was challenging at best and humiliating at worst. Not only was I huge in my homemade maternity clothes as I attended a state college in California (where every co-ed was blond and gorgeous in her halter top) but every time we discussed some strange primitive custom surrounding fertility, my professor would say, "Isn't that true, Mrs. Heskin?"

My education was terribly important to me, and so Neil made it terribly important to him. Lots of evenings he completely took over baths and bedtime for our sons because I had a paper to write. When I had a night class, he supervised cooking (or ordered pizza). His love made it possible for me to realize a dream. Most importantly, he never complained, and only occasionally mentioned the laundry. More often he had the laundry done when I got home.

One thing about education is that it forces you to change and grow. Sometimes these changes can be hard for a marriage to absorb, especially when one partner doesn't support or care about what is happening to the other. I was very lucky. When I began graduate studies in ministry, it was clear that I was changing. Neil and I talked about my classes often. He said it was important for him to know what was happening to me. I would come home from class, and after supper we'd take a glass of wine into the living room, and I would share my notes from a class on Scripture or spirituality. Although we don't always share the same interests, I guess this coming together was significant because it wasn't long before Neil signed up for classes too.

I can love Neil unconditionally when he needs time and space to sort things out. He likes to gather information, to read and explore possibilities when there is a project to do. I am impatient to get things done, and I love the fact that I am intuitive by nature. Just recently we had some remodeling done to our home. Actually I had wanted to do this for several years, but because of a crazy roof line and several unstoppable leaks, the work was going to be quite extensive. Neil knew we would have to do the work eventually, but he wanted to be careful. I can outtalk Neil easily, and probably could have pushed hard to begin on my schedule, but I made a decision to move at his pace and not to plunge in and get going. I also did not criticize or cajole to get my way, even though these techniques have worked pretty well for me in the past. The work was finished a month ago, and I am still so excited about how it turned out. It is beautiful, and in fact, the design is better than my original idea. Loving Neil unconditionally in this experience gave us a bonus, and taught me more about trying to share his world.

Couples who work at loving unconditionally allow themselves to be changed by the other. They may not share the same work, or study the same things, but they can support each other and see value in their different paths. Their unconditional love is a hint of the kind of love God has for us, the faith community. That kind of love may be countercultural, but it is the kind of love that will transform us.

Consensus and interdependence

Another gift that married couples can share with the community is their ability and their willingness to come to consensus. Today businesses and even parishes are hiring expensive consultants to help them deal with collaborative issues, when they could just look to strong married couples who make consensus a way of life. Consensus is learned through trial and error, often through the discovery that making decisions independently causes pain. The hardest part of consensus thinking for me was with money. (Actually, it still is!) In my family there was enough money to go around, and I thought that was still true after we got married. Several times I spent money that we couldn't afford on things I thought I couldn't live without. It was hard for Neil, the account-ant, to find himself "in the red" at the end of the month. He, on the other hand, sometimes found it hard to spend money on going out to dinner, and could wait indefinitely for a chair or end table we needed. And he still doesn't know why anyone would need five different pairs of black shoes. Our different views about money have caused a lot of tension between us, but we have worked hard to try to understand each other's values. This effort has changed both of us. I have learned to pay attention to our budget, and Neil has learned not to squirrel every dollar away.

Neil especially had trouble with consensus in decision-making. When we had been married six years, Neil's job required a lot of travel; often he'd leave on Monday and return Friday evening. One week when he was in California, I missed him a lot. When I picked him up at the airport, I suggested that we skip the party we were going to and just go home together. He replied, "I think we should go to the party because we probably will not see these people again." Then he told me that he had accepted a job in Los Angeles and that we were moving the next month. I hadn't even known he was offered the job. I felt all the blood drain out of my face. I was shocked, devastated, and angry. I felt as though Neil hadn't even considered how going to California would affect me. For me, moving meant quitting my job, leaving school, and, most difficult of all, cancelling our adoption plans and beginning again when we got to California. Moving for Neil meant a great promo-tion, a new beginning, and living in a place where he had always wanted to live. Neil's job was our main income, and he felt that gave him the right to make decisions concerning work. It was the early 70's, and I had been taught the same thing, but I was over-whelmed by the effect his decision had on me. Nevertheless, like a "good wife" I swallowed my feelings and went. It was one of the hardest things I ever had to do. Needless to say, Neil and I have had lots of discussions since then about the effect of independent decisions. We both had to learn to collaborate more on how we used our resources and how we moved through our life. In a culture that values rugged individualism, we have made a conscious choice to be a "we" in all of our decisions.

The kind of consensus I speak of is not arguing until one gives up or gives in. It is a sharing of two distinct value systems to create a new set of shared values unique to each particular relationship. It is a blending of the best of each person, which doesn't swallow up individuality but rather creates an atmosphere where persons can be fully themselves. It is carrying the other in our hearts. Every time I go to the grocery store, I carry my family with me, not necessarily in the car but in my heart. I don't have to ask what each one likes, what favorite foods I should get. They are part of my life. Every decision I make about work and social engagements requires that I weigh carefully everyone's needs in addition to my own. Sometimes I can consult, asking how this conference or that trip to the city will affect everyone's schedules. But even when that is not possible, my decisions are based on the fact that I belong to this family.

A husband and wife plan their careers by sharing with each other the fears, hopes, anxieties, and challenges that surround any decisions. By listening to each other they learn how these things affect their spouse. Young couples may leave behind the ways their families of origin celebrated Christmas to create new traditions and rituals for themselves. There is a testing and sorting that takes place in early marriage in order to find common ground. It takes time to make the other person an integral part of your life. Couples have to learn to make decisions that are for the good of the whole. When they do, they call us, the community of believers, to carry one another in our hearts in the same way. They remind us that the way we choose to live profoundly affects others.

Loving conflict and reconciliation

The third gift or grace in marriage is the ability to forgive. God's love for us is also revealed when a married couple willingly enters into the chaos of conflict to fight for the sake of their relationship and then struggles to forgive each other. Through the separating and coming together, in the brokenness and healing that takes place in marriage, God's faithfulness to God's people takes flesh. But fighting did not come easily for Neil and me. In my family fighting was painful, and in Neil's family fighting meant long silences. We had to learn to fight well, in fact, to care enough about each other to fight at all. Sometimes we caused pain and had to wade through that pain to find each other. Then we had to work to forgive. It is because Neil and I have been able to forgive each other that we can say anything at all about marriage. We will never have all our differences resolved. I will continue to hurt him, to be critical instead of supportive, to fail to love, and so will he. Because we have hurt each other deeply in our life together, we know how to ask for forgiveness. And we have learned to risk saying things that are painful and to trust that we will be heard.

For ten years beginning in 1982, Neil and I worked together, which gave us ample opportunity to practice forgiving one another! As Dickens once said, "It was the best of times, it was the worst of times." The worst of times occurred when we didn't listen. The store we owned had grown, and Neil knew we needed to buy a computer. But he knew not to make that decision alone, and so he explained to me all the reasons why a computer would make life so much easier. I tried to listen but couldn't hear him over the terrible fears I had about computers in general, and about owning our own in particular. Now fear is not rational, and Neil was very patient. He waited for me to work through my roadblock, all the while accumulating data and magazines about computers, which he shared with me eagerly. I did not budge.

Finally Neil ordered "it." We were going to a trade show the next week, and he was really hopeful that I would get excited about the computer when I saw it displayed at the show. Our usual routine at this show was to separate and go to the various booths, meeting for lunch and dinner to compare notes. Each time we met, Neil would ask if I had had a chance to try out the computer. "No, I was at the other end of the hall" or, "I never had a minute" only went so far. He made an appointment for me to meet with the representative the next day. I swear I didn't mean to be late for that appointment—at least consciously. When I showed up twenty minutes late, Neil was breathing fire. I went up to the technician, asked her how to turn on the computer, and then how to turn it off. I thanked her and walked away.

I can't remember Neil and me ever being so mad at each other. The subject was so tender that we did not even refer to it when we met for dinner. We talked about inconsequential things, carefully avoiding any mention of technology. We went to a lovely restaurant in Anaheim, California, city of thousands of restaurants. We were halfway through our salad when the maitre d' seated a couple facing us. Unbelievably, it was the computer technician and her assistant! And that was the end of our truce. We left without finishing our dinner and went back to the hotel to have the fight.

We were so far apart that it took a long time to bridge the distance so we could hear each other. I knew in my heart that Neil was right, we definitely needed the computer. But he wasn't listening to the fears I had about spending so much money (I had learned from the best), and even less clear, the fear that one day I would somehow hit the wrong button and cause our entire inventory to crash. I have a phobia about mechanical things and am convinced that machines can actually smell fear. It may be hard for younger people to understand, but moving into the computer age was extremely difficult for lots of old folks! Neil was angry that I had disregarded him on this subject, even to the point of showing up late for the appointment and dismissing him and the technician. The words came slowly at first, and then gushed out. I felt uncomfortable and a little stupid telling Neil how I felt about the computer. He said he didn't know it went that deep. He said how upset he was that I blew off the appointment he had set up, and he believed me when I told him it was an accident. We finally heard each other and sought a way to show our respect and love. The trust we had was damaged by the way we had both acted, but our willingness to forgive went a long way to restoring that trust.

There is a covenant in marriage upon which couples may rely, which gives them freedom to enter wholeheartedly into the struggle and to count on the presence of God's grace to help heal the hurts that are caused. The promise of partners to share a lifetime offers the opportunity to not only heal and forgive the hurts that occur in their own marriage, but also to journey together to heal and forgive hurts that are part of their past and that get in the way of loving fully. This gift, when it is shared well, is a powerful witness to the healing power of God in relationship. The children of such a marriage are aware of God's continual desire to forgive us.

Imaging God's love

The wedding ritual hints at that mystery, which is probably why we all celebrate weddings so passionately. Any mother-of-the-bride can tell you how much energy goes into planning the celebration. The account of the wedding at Cana should prompt couples to invite Jesus to be part of their celebration, so that when their joy runs out he can refill them again abundantly. The wedding itself is only a beginning, sort of a kingdom promise...here but not yet; just as Cana was a hint, a glimpse of what God is and was doing in the world, in Jesus.

At its heart matrimony is a community sacrament. The bride and groom are the celebrants of the marriage ritual, witnessed by the priest who stands for the entire community. The ritual calls the community to journey with the couple. The fruits of the sacrament come through a lifetime of work and love. In St. Paul's letter to the Ephesians he tells us that the relationship of husband and wife is like the relationship of Christ and the church; that the love a married couple reveals is the love that God has for God's people. This privilege of revealing the love of God is both overwhelming and empowering. God's love is passionate and abundant, and that is reflected in a couple's passion for one another. The intimacy enjoyed in marriage is sexual, emotional, and spiritual, and it depends on self-giving.

It is difficult to speak of the love of a married couple without recognizing that this love calls them to share in God's creative love as parents. But the sacrament of matrimony is not the sacrament of parenthood. In the Vatican II document *Gaudium et Spes*, we read that it is the mutual gift of two persons, their intimate union, as well as the good of the children, that argues for unbreakable oneness in the relationship. Parenthood in marriage flows from the love of a wife for her husband and a husband for his wife, from their mutual gift of self to the other. The willingness to bring life through each other and to mutually share in the work of nurturing that life to adulthood stands as a challenge to us, the community of believers. The witness of that commitment to belong to each other and to their children calls us to ask "To whom do we belong?" It leads us, the community, to respond by turning outward from ourselves. But as important as parenthood is, it is not the only way life is given. Couples are called to make their relationship a creative force that will be life-giving to each other and to the community. This is not an inward love, but a love that expands to embrace the rest of the people of God.

As married couples deepen their understanding of relationship, it would be helpful if the church invited them to share that understanding with a community that has serious questions about intimacy and relationships between men and women. The authority with which married couples may speak comes from years of struggling with these questions in their relationships. They have an authority that can help to heal a culture inundated with broken relationships aired and exploited on talk shows. They offer an alternative to a culture that presents marriage as serial monogamy. Most importantly they understand that matrimony is not a thing that a couple receives on their wedding day, but rather something that a couple becomes. I learned to be wife from Neil, and he learned to be husband from me. Our marriage is not just two individuals joined together but two persons who discover a new way of living because they are together. It is that new creation born of our relationship that continues to give us life.

Sacramental marriage comes in choosing each day to live an ordinary life in an extraordinary way, which is the spiritual path of marriage. Couples who choose this life make it possible for the community to understand God's presence. The choosing is not just for the major events of birth, illness, or death, but for the little things that require a daily dying to self; for example, a wife getting up to put coffee on when she'd rather sleep in, or a husband chatting at breakfast when the sports section is much more inviting. Choosing this life requires that both of them affirm instead of criticize, and allow laughter to end a quarrel instead of insisting on being right. This kind of love means being vulnerable, and it calls for sharing hurts instead of hiding them and being independent. When a married couple lives this way, they invite the community to nourish a deeper understanding of one another, an understanding that doesn't give up, that looks for the gifts in each member and affirms those gifts, drawing them out for the good of the community.

And so the bride and groom say yes to mystery hidden in unaccustomed jars, disguised as water, waiting to be transformed, meant to be tasted, created to be shared.

Reflection Questions

1. John Dunne said: "The way of necessity and the way of possibility turned out to be the same way." In what way is marriage the way of possibility?

2. How does loving unconditionally open you to being changed by another?

3. Three qualities of marriage are unconditional love, coming to consensus, and active forgiving. What are the obstacles to these in you? What is revealed when you try to live these qualities?

4. How has God's abundance transformed your life?

Two

Watching the Road

Prodigals and Promise

When he came to himself, the son said, "I will get up and go to my father, and I will say to him, 'Father, I have sinned against heaven and before you; I am no longer worthy to be called your son'"…. While he was still far off, his father saw him and was filled with compassion; he ran and put his arms around him and kissed him.

—Luke 15:11–32

On our twenty-fifth wedding anniversary, Neil and I celebrated with our faith community during a Mass at our parish. We renewed our vows and we threw a party afterwards. As we had dreamed about how we would mark that milestone, we thought of all the friends in our community, people with whom we had celebrated, mourned, worked, laughed, wept, held our breath, prayed, sung, and shared bread and life, for almost twenty years. We had discovered our place in the church as we had gathered each week with this community. We couldn't imagine leaving anyone out of our festivities, so we brought a brunch to that holy place.

Just by chance the reading that Sunday was the parable of the prodigal son, and it probably wasn't chance at all. Neil and I listened to the story of the son who took his inheritance and squandered it. The story is often applied to parents and children, but as I listened, I heard our marriage journey in the story. I remembered that once when our son Tom was about ten, he had commented on this gospel story. He said, "You know, the father did not just happen to be there the day the son came home. Every day he went out to the road and watched." In many ways this is what happens in marriage, we become road watchers. I found the reading to be incredibly appropriate and fitting for a commitment to life together, yet I have never heard it read at a wedding. Marriage is a series of comings and goings, of changes in behavior and thinking, of giving up and then starting over. According to Jewish tradition, when God created humans, God gave them a secret, and that secret was not how to begin but how to begin again. Marriage involves growing…sometimes apart and hopefully together again, seeking and giving forgiveness, not taking these things for granted but celebrating when they happen. Love demands that we stand by the road every day watching for each other, welcoming each other home. And this teaches us to welcome others, our parents, our children, when they have not met our expectations, or have hurt us. When two people choose to live this way, their marriage becomes a way of expressing the paschal mystery of dying and rising in their everyday life.

During our anniversary Mass, as I listened to Fr. Rich talk about forgiveness, I realized that being married to Neil had taught me to stand in a place of forgiveness. In fact, reconciliation is the most critical work of the first years of marriage, and, if you do it well, it becomes the work of a lifetime. Each of us comes to relationships with broken places inside us, things we may not even consciously remember but that affect our ability to love. To become fully human is to be on the journey toward becoming whole, that is, on a journey toward healing and forgiveness. To be married is to have the possibility of having a companion to share that journey, someone who will help us dig a little deeper, someone who will cause us to reflect on our behavior. Because of the things that Neil and I encountered on our road together, I have learned to forgive myself, my parents, uncontrolled events, God, our children, and Neil. I am getting better at it, too.

Revisiting my life

The first, forgiving myself, is actually the foundation piece. If the prodigal son had been unable to get up out of the pigsty of his isolation, he could never have moved toward reconciliation. My own self-doubt, my lack of kindness to me about my flaws is that pigsty. If I choose to wallow, I have nothing to give. When I see God with us...with me...I see the Incarnation as an ongoing event...I am able to move. Then all the pieces of my life, reflected upon and blessed, are all that I have to bring to Neil.

The story of the prodigal and his journey home still reflects much of our life. I can find Neil and me in each person in the story, and I understand the value that reconciliation holds for us. Our years together have smoothed some of our rough edges, taught us to be patient when we cannot yet forgive, healed some deep hurts, given us understanding of our parents and their lives, and moved us toward blessing all of it. These years of learning to love and be loved, have given me the gift of seeing my life through different eyes.

Unlike the father of the prodigal, I was not always that forgiving. When I was a child I often wished my parents were more fun. I had to learn painfully how to "wait by the road for them." Because we lived near New York City there was an infinite number of things to do, but we didn't do many of them. My friends' families did lots of things that I wished for in my family. Joanne Donnelly's parents took her to see plays like *Camelot* and *My Fair Lady*. My parents went themselves but they did not take me, even though I asked to go. Kathy Woods' dad was a riot. He told great jokes and acted silly. Nobody acted silly at my house, though I wished they would. Well, once, at a family picnic, Daddy lined all the cousins up and had us face the clothesline. We each had an enormous, drippy slice of watermelon, and the object was to spit the pits over the line. On the count of three we all turned and spit the pits at Daddy. I have a vivid picture of him, after his initial surprise, laughing together with my mother. I treasure that memory because laughter didn't happen very often in my family.

Kathy Sillaway's mom let us play "Princess" and gave us ball gowns to wear. Nancy Bowman's father built a puppet stage with lights and curtains and real marionettes. My parents were very busy, and although I wished they would have, they didn't play much with us. Except during hurricanes. As soon as the lights would go out (which they did every time we got a great wind), we'd go next door to Aunt Jean's house, and Mom and I and Aunt Jean and Susan would play canasta by candle light. The world seemed to be only as large as the circle of the light from the candles, and I felt safe, even with the wind howling outside. I still like storms because they remind me of the gift of safety, security, and friends.

Other children's parents went to their games, drove them places, told them stories, took vacations together. I went to camp all summer from the time I was ten. While I was gone, my parents would rent a summer house at the end of Long Island. I loved camp, in fact it was the only peaceful place I remember from childhood, but I missed my family.

Other children's dads helped with homework, took their side against the world, told them stories. I was sick a lot as a child, in bed for a few months when I was seven. One night my Dad told me a wonderful story of Cinderella in her XKE. It was a magical tale, mostly because I felt so close to him and loved. I asked if he would tell me another the next night, and he said "yes." The following night he told me he owed me one, the next night two. I stopped counting at three hundred forty. Other dads didn't drink too much, didn't work all the time, had conversations about dreams and ideas, not just business.

Other children's moms thought their children were good and told them sometimes. It was not my mother's way. When our oldest child was two, my mother overheard me praising him for something he had done. She grabbed my arm and said, "Don't ever give a child a compliment, it will make him conceited." Other moms took their daughters shopping and then out to lunch in Marshall Field. I remember shopping trips when I would find a dress I loved, we would buy it, then while I was at school the next day mom would return it to the store. I began to rip the tags off in the car on the way home. Other children's moms were happy, wanted to live, didn't try to take their lives. They passed on what it means to be a woman, instead of feelings of fear and shame. My mother told me she wanted to die.

I guess I wanted other children's parents.

Unlike the prodigal son who traveled to a different land, I only ventured six blocks away to my cousins' house. I was always welcome at my Aunt Lillian and Uncle Jim's, and even though they had five children of their own, they always seemed glad I came. Their home was happy and alive, and nobody minded noise or clutter. But most of all, Aunt Lillian would listen to me. In high school I left home as often as I could, beginning to work as a nurse's aide as soon as I was fifteen. Before that, in grammar school I would leave home and go to Kathy Shea's house after school. Her mom would give me a cup of tea, which made me feel very grown up. We would sit at her kitchen table like a couple of old friends, with her caring about what was important to me.

I left home even before that as a little girl of five, to ride my bike away, away. I loved to play in the clay pits about a quarter mile away from my home. I could only ride my bike part way, then I would leave it and walk through bushes and tangles to an open space. If it had rained recently there would be wonderful slimy clay, and I would sit for hours and fashion beautiful works of art. I didn't bring them home because my home was very clean, and the clay was very messy. There was a wonderful woods near the clay pits, and I would swing on a vine out over a deep ravine. I recently went back to that place and discovered that the ravine is only seven feet deep, but to my little body then it seemed bottomless.

I remember as a little girl lying on my back looking through branches at the sky, sitting on other people's lawns, helping Mrs. Cridlin clean her house. Mrs. Cridlin lived eight houses away, and she had a wondrous house with white pillars, filled with antiques that she let me touch. She had a 1936 Packard, maroon with lots of chrome, sitting in her garage. The interior of that car felt as big as a living room, with plush upholstery and foldaway seats. She let Susan Field (my best friend from next door) and me sit in the car whenever we wanted to, and once in a while she would take us for a drive. In the dining room of Mrs. Cridlin's house was a bell under a rug by the head of the table, and if you stepped on it you could summon the servants (long since gone) from the kitchen. She would let Susan and me ring it, and then would bring us cookies and Coke, and we would be so elegant. In exchange we would do her "spring cleaning," which consisted of a light dusting and two swipes of the vacuum. I loved to visit her because she let me have free run of the house. At my house I remember playing in my closet so I didn't make a mess.

A companion on the road

When I met Neil, I left home for good. The first step was from New York to New Jersey. Not far enough? Then we moved to California, and finally settled for a compromise in Illinois. It was during those moves that we became parents. Busy with work, far from home, like the prodigal son I realized that I could only bring to my children all the life that had happened to me. If I didn't become aware of who I was, there would only be corn husks for our children to feed upon. I realized that in the same way our parents had brought their life experiences to us. We were doing our best, and our parents had done their best too. I knew I couldn't give my boys what I had not known, so I had to try to learn it. I began to watch the road, faithfully every day, and Neil watched with me. We walked back over our lives, and shared the things that hurt us. They seemed easier, somehow, for having a companion on the road. We teased out the good parts, and were glad for the ways they formed us. We tried to find meaning in the pain. It was not easy, but it was good work. As we observed our past together, we healed each other and opened ourselves to forgiveness. Once our son Paul asked me if I had ever wished I had different parents. I asked him why. He told me he had often imagined what it would have been like if my parents had told me I was good and encouraged me more. He also said he didn't wish that any more because who I am and what I understand is all part of that. His words told me I had been able to bless the prodigal in me—and in them.

I began to watch other places, other roads—at parties, when friends gathered, other dads and daughters. I watched at Marshall Field's luncheonette, other moms and daughters. I watched in the car, riding in silence, looking for a glimpse. Late at night or early in the morning, I detected a whisper. In the soft or hard places in my soul, I felt forgiveness.

Until one day, from high on the hill, in the same way the father saw his son at a distance, I spotted an old, bent couple, broken/healing, tentative/knowing. And I ran, arms reaching, heart bursting, to gather them as they were, not the other children's parents that I had wished for, but my parents, the ones I had always needed.

This understanding, this reflection, was the best gift of our silver anniversary.

Reflection questions

1. Each of us comes to relationship with broken places. What are the broken places in your childhood that keep you from loving fully?

2. What experiences in adolescence keep you from trusting?

3. How has your relationship helped you to heal these broken places?

4. How can you stand, as the Prodigal Father did, in a place of reconciliation?

THREE

Celebrating Our Differences

You Say Tomato, I Say Tomahto

Now as they went on their way, Jesus entered a certain village, where a woman named Martha welcomed him into her home. She had a sister named Mary, who sat at the Lord's feet and listened to what he was saying.

—Luke 10:38–42

When someone begins a sentence with "There are two kinds of people…" I immediately know two things: First, it will be easy to tell which kind that person is by the smallest hint of disdain used to categorize the other. And second, I know that—almost inevitably—Neil and I will be one of each. It has been that way since we met, and dealing with differences has not been without challenge.

There are two kinds of people.... Morning and night; spenders and savers; introverts and extroverts; neat and "relaxed" (note my bias); talkative and quiet; detail-oriented and global. And that about describes us. There is a personality indicator called Myers Briggs, with eight possible letters that identify certain traits. Each letter describes a way of behaving or viewing the world. Many couples share at least one or two letters. Neil and I each have our own separate set of four: he is ISTJ and I am ENFP. Therefore we approach every decision, each issue from opposite ends with different styles and preferences, and somehow we try to meet in the middle.

What sometimes makes this meeting in the middle difficult is our stubborn insistence on our own style. For example, there are two kinds of people, those who like the story in Scripture of Martha and Mary, when Mary is sitting at the feet of Jesus and Martha wants some help with the meal, and those who think Jesus was rather unkind to Martha when he told her that Mary had chosen the better part. I personally think it is a great story. Not being terribly concerned about details, I can't imagine fussing in the kitchen when you could be sitting and talking. I have been known to step over a laundry basket on the landing and truly not see it, while Neil has been known to spend hours picking dead leaves out of the cracks in the deck with a scraper. Even at mealtimes we can only simultaneously enjoy the part with the food. I like to sit and talk afterwards, while Neil jumps up to get the dishes done. Well, one day I read the story of the two sisters a little differently. You see, it is Martha who asks the question, "Lord do you not care that my sister has left me by myself to do the serving?" And so Jesus needed to answer her. I started to wonder what would have happened if Mary had asked a similar question.

As they continued their journey Jesus entered a village where Neil and Kathy welcomed him. When their meal was finished, Neil jumped up from the table to clear the dishes. He turned on the coffee pot (which Kathy had forgotten). There was a spill on the floor which would be tracked on the rugs, so he wiped it up. The phone rang—someone selling insurance—and he was gracious to the caller, taking what seemed like an inordinately long time. As he scraped, rinsed, and stacked the dishes, Kathy found herself getting more and more impatient. In fact, she could hardly listen to what Jesus was saying because she couldn't believe Neil was missing the most important part of the visit...again. He really ought to learn to relax and sit down, to let the work take care of itself.

Kathy said to Jesus, "Don't you care that my husband cannot stop working to spend time with you?" And Jesus got up, went into the kitchen, and helped Neil load the dishwasher.

See? It depends on who asks the question. We all get the answer we need to hear.

Differences: opportunities or stumbling blocks

Whomever we marry, these questions will be raised. We can count on there being several, or many, opposing traits and preferences. The potential for greatness or disaster in that kind of mating is enormous. Differences can be an opportunity for wholeness and healing, offering us a chance to walk back through our life with a different set of eyes, and to experience ourselves and our behavior through one another. Or differences can be a source of ongoing conflict because of dug-in heels, insistence on being right, unwillingness to bend, or an inability to listen to another and be changed. It's a choice. Pick one.

I have attended dozens of weddings, and every marriage begins happily ever after. It's only later that disintegration starts. In our ministry to engaged couples Neil and I have been privileged to help many couples prepare for the sacrament of matrimony. Despite enormous differences in the lifestyles, ages, backgrounds, and skills of the couples, each one shared one common trait: incredible optimism about their coming life together. When we would question couples on possible problems because of their differences, or possible disappointments that might occur in their life, nearly all of them fully trusted their ability to meet and overcome those challenges. I remember one couple very well. Every time we asked a question, she answered. We staged questions for the man, used all of our body language skills to include him in the conversation, and still she answered. It would have been funny if it weren't so sad. Finally, I sat with my back to her, leaned over toward him, and said, "Joe, how does it feel when every time I ask you a question, Judy answers?" Over my shoulder I heard her say, "He doesn't mind."

The scariest part of this story is that I could relate to it. Neil is quiet and very willing to let me talk for both of us. I delight in conversations, debates, even arguments, and can use my words and his words against him. Neil has expressed frustration when we fight because he feels he cannot say anything right, or anything I won't be able to use against him. We spent a lot of time that evening talking with the couple about what we observed. Neil told them how he feels when I don't invite his opinion or don't listen to him when he gives it. At that point in their relationship they saw not fighting as a good thing. Her interruptions bothered him, but he loved her way too much to tell her. We tried to let them know that loving someone means you are obliged to tell them what you feel. We also told them that while this might not be a problem now, it would be someday, and to call us whenever they hit the wall. We haven't heard from them yet, but we will always be here if they need us.

Even with particularly severe differences in personality and values, couples profess a strong belief in their ability to handle any situation that might arise. To them love will conquer all, and it is inconceivable that anything will destroy that love. Reality often comes as a great surprise to many newly married couples, but is also the fertile soil where they can learn about themselves, each other, and who they can be. In bringing together differences, there is a possibility of a whole that is greater than its parts. And it is worth all the work!

I can understand their optimism, though, because when I fell in love with Neil I felt it too. I was blissfully unconcerned that we had vastly dissimilar backgrounds, personalities, values, and preferences. And I believe that this optimism, this stubborn belief in each other, is right even in the face of great challenges. What I didn't understand when we vowed to love each other was that the abundance of God's grace would be with us. That understanding came with living.

That first, single step

Neil and I first met as we walked out of the cafeteria one night when we were in college in Washington, D.C. Neil played on the basketball team, and I was in nursing school. The ball players had late practices and the nursing students had late anatomy lab, so we often ate dinner together as a large group. In the crowd walking out that night, Neil and I were separated from the group and ended up walking side by side. Neil was so quiet that I started babbling about how beautiful the Washington Monument was, all lit up in the snow across the river. I mentioned that I would like to go there (meaning some day). Neil, being a kind sort of person, thought I was asking him out (not done in those days) and, to save me embarrassment, asked if I wanted to go. I realized my mistake, thought fast, and said, "If we go we have to walk" (hoping he would politely decline). Neil, who had no money and no car, thought this was a great idea.

And so we started out on foot, for the wrong reasons, trying to be nice, not knowing why or how we would get where we were going. We began a journey of two miles and more than thirty years, exchanging information about ourselves, admiring the view, wondering about this other person, coming closer together...and this is what we still do.

In our first few months together, we discovered we had totally different backgrounds, that our parents had raised us quite differently, and that we had opposite views on money (Neil liked to squirrel it away and invest; I had no idea where it went and my checking account overdrew into my father's). And that was only the beginning. Our study habits were different. (Neil had to budget time because his commitment to the basketball team required him to spend hours a day practicing, while I could easily put aside books if anything else was going on.) Even the things we liked were at odds. Neil knew every team, player, and record in nearly every sport, and I couldn't imagine why anyone would care about those things. But Neil had so many wonderful qualities, we just seemed to fit. I was pretty disorganized; the word my father used most often was "skippy." Neil was organized, steady, and got things done. I admired it because it complemented me so well.

And at five-feet, nine inches tall, always the second-to-last girl in line at school events (I still bless Mary Ann Hicks for her extra inch), I was delighted that Neil was six-feet, nine inches tall in his stocking feet. In fact, I immediately went out and bought five pairs of spiked heels, navy, black, tan, red, and white. I was ready for all seasons within a week of meeting him. I felt secure with Neil, and I liked the feeling. He enjoyed my enthusiasm for life, my excitement with people, my ability to talk to strangers. Both of us filled in gaps in the other, and I thought it was perfect.

Nothing could spoil the love we had. Our differences weren't anything to worry about, and no one else seemed to worry either. Our parents had no objections, my friends loved Neil, and his liked me. When we decided to marry, our marriage preparation was fairly typical for the late sixties. We met a couple of times with the priest in my parish, and he said a few things about marriage for a lifetime and a lot about children, and then he and Neil talked about basketball. Even though Fr. Hoffman was very aware of my mother's mental illness and my father's problems with alcohol, he never discussed how these things might have affected me or my ability to enter into a relationship. There was an old Irish saying, "Don't air your dirty laundry in public," and so I didn't, not even to Neil. He had some laundry piled up in the back of his closet, too.

A few bumps in the road
With that beginning, it should not be surprising that we ran into trouble in those first years of marriage. One of the things about Neil that first attracted me was his Gary Cooper strong silent image. That and the fact that he was reliable and steady. I was just a little wild, and I saw him helping me to be grounded. It didn't take long before grounded felt like being in the ground—buried. Reliable had a definite twinge of anal retentive, with all of our bills

in alphabetized folders, in chronological order. Neil was strong
and silent, to be sure. Having a conversation was like pulling
teeth. I had to remind myself not to ask questions that could be
answered by one word.

I knew that once Neil and I were married he would want to do
things my way more and more. For instance, when I was growing
up, we ate dinner in the dining room, with linen and silver. One
of my early memories is of setting the table, and I would recite,
"Cream-sugar-pepper-salt-bread-butter-knives-forks-spoons-butter
plates-butter knives" as I set about my job. My family would all
talk, especially when I was younger and things hadn't fallen apart
just yet. I remember during the meal getting the dictionary to look
up words. My father had a wonderful vocabulary, and would say
things just so my brother and I would ask what he meant. He also
could teach simply by the way he used words. I remember saying
something nasty to my brother, and hearing Daddy say, "That was
vile, vicious, vindictive, and vituperative." It was pretty clear I was
in trouble. Or he would mention a topic and we'd have to get
Volume A of the encyclopedia to look up African history or
anthracite coal. It was lots of fun. In Neil's house dinner hinged
on the stock report and the sports report. Nobody talked, or they
might miss a closing price or a score. I was absolutely sure Neil
would prefer my way of eating, and I was absolutely wrong.

Neil, on the other hand, seemed a bit unreasonable about how I
handled the "little things" like the checkbook and the charge cards.
I remember just before our wedding, he asked me if I had the bank
reconciliations for my account for the preceding year. I was quite
proud of the fact that I did, and I gave them to him, in their original envelopes, unopened. He thought it was cute and patiently
explained how and why you reconcile checks each month. (I had

thought that was the reason you paid a service charge to the bank.) After we were married a while, he thought it was less cute, and he was much less patient. In fact, he was frustrated.

I think our biggest difference and difficulty came from the fact that I am way out there as an extrovert, and Neil is really introverted. I used to believe that everything would be great if he would just learn to think the way I did, after all it was so much friendlier to be an extrovert. When we had something to discuss, I wanted to discuss! Extroverts need to chew things over and listen to themselves in order to know what they are thinking. Neil could not stand the fact that I might begin at one point and end up in an entirely different place. He, on the other hand, never said a word until he had checked out all the facts and weighed all the possibilities. It was years before we understood that neither of us was crazy, only different, and that both styles of thinking were good! Trial and error taught us how to turn these differences into strengths.

Both of us came from families that didn't deal with conflict too well, and neither did we. I tended to cry at tense moments, and Neil tended to withdraw. My own expectations of marriage were highly romantic, while Neil's were excessively practical. I once asked him what he thought the role of a husband was. He said it was to provide a good home for the children. At the time I had been going through tests for infertility, and his answer hurt deeply. I asked him what he thought *his* role was, since we apparently couldn't have children. He had no answer. If we had been the couple in "Can This Marriage Be Saved," a call-in vote would have been strongly on the side of "no." Apparently the marriage counselor we located in the Yellow Pages didn't think we could be saved either because he told us that Neil and I were completely unsuited for each other, and that we should get divorced before we had kids.

And so one evening Neil and I found ourselves talking about who got what furniture. He could have the bed, it was extra-long, and I would take the sofa, I liked the fabric. He didn't care about the silver and china, and I cared disproportionately. Neil estimated our legal and court fees at about $1,500, and I pointed out, "For $1,500 we could go to Europe." And Neil, quite out of his ordinary, asked, "Do you want to go?" We did! That was our first experience of grace in our marriage. I am forever grateful that we were open to it.

A series of new beginnings

Neil and I came home from Europe the same two different people, with the same life and challenges but with a new perspective. We began to try to appreciate our differences. God has been extremely creative in making each of us unique. No two people have the same fingerprints. In fact, I recently heard that no two people have the same ear, and I have been checking ears ever since. I think it is true. Everyone's genetic make-up is different, and additionally, each of us has a value system, personality, and style that cannot be duplicated. As a matter of fact, Neil and I married each other because we enjoyed our differences, and then spent enormous amounts of energy trying to make each other into our own image and likeness! The very things that were enchanting in the beginning became stumbling blocks when we let them. What was steady and secure could become static and boring, and what was bubbly and enthusiastic could be seen as air-headed and irresponsible. It's all in the perspective. To make our differences work for us, Neil and I had to remember why these differences had made us fall in love in the first place. We also had to realize that just because we see things differently, it is not a choice between good and bad, right and wrong. Both of our sets of values, both of our styles, both of our ways of being, were right for us as individuals. What we needed was to learn to share them.

Holding different values doesn't make one or the other wrong. The work of marriage is to find values that belong to both of you. I compare it to the early pioneers who set out across the country in a covered wagon. They crammed into the wagon everything they thought they would need for the life they were seeking. But it wasn't very long before it began to feel crowded in the wagon, and things that had seemed essential no longer fit. And so they tossed them out the back. I have heard it was not uncommon to see a trunk of fancy dresses, or a piano, or a horsehair sofa jettisoned along the westward trail. Sometimes the settlers discovered they had forgotten some tool or utensil that was needed, and they had to fashion it out of what they had. The pioneers also brought some things with them that to others might have no value, but they kept these things as treasures because the objects spoke of who they were. On our trip to Europe Neil and I bought one of the gaudy alabaster statues of "The Kiss." We keep it in our bedroom to remind us of how fragile and precious our love is. We also keep it in our room because it was too embarrassing to our children to have it in the living room. It is one of our treasures. The sifting through, tossing out the back, and rigging new things continues along the whole journey. When the early settlers finally reached their destination, they had what they actually needed. And so will we.

Each one of us comes to our marriage crammed full of preferences, values we think we will need on our journey, like the way dinner is served (or not), where and when vacations are taken, how decisions about money are made, how to celebrate holidays. It's interesting that values connected to holidays are often the most closely held values. We knew a couple who took this to extremes. His mother had always put the lights on the Christmas tree, and her father had always done that job. On their first Christmas they chopped down their tree, brought it home and set it up, and waited...and waited. Each thought the other should put the lights on, each one dug in their heels and decided to wait for the other. That year the tree stood bare, without any decoration at all. They have gotten past the hurt of that Christmas, but the memory helps them to put arguments into perspective. Whenever one or the other gets really stubborn, they only have to say, "Remember the tree!"

Somehow, in the whirlwind of the first few years of marriage, couples must choose values that will work for both of them, a little from each, or something entirely new. Things will get tossed out the back of the wagon, and it will be so much more comfortable riding.

Most of the time couples don't even realize they are doing this. And suddenly there will be a moment of clarity. We had one recently. Neil and I both love to canoe. For both of us, taking the canoe out into the quiet of early morning, before the jet skis destroy the peace of the bay, is magical.

Neil loves to go close to the shore, to look at all of the rocks and plants, to see if there are any eggs in the nests along the shoreline, to spy turtles perched on trees that have fallen into the water. I like to go way out, to look at the wide expanse of trees and shore, of sky and water, as a whole. Two very different canoe rides. I noticed, however, the last time we went out for our ride, I instinctively headed for the bank and looked for the baby ducks we had seen the week before. They had left the nest. Two more trees were down and would be carried into the river during the next storm. We skirted the shore, exploring until it was time to go home for breakfast. It wasn't until Neil paddled way out in the bay that we headed for home. He said how lovely the woods looked in that light. He was caught by the beauty of the whole scene.

It seems that through our sharing of different views, we have enlarged both of our worlds. And it is a much more interesting canoe ride.

Reflection questions

1. Name the most challenging differences in your relationship.

2. Which differences are a source of tension? Which differences are a source of delight?

3. Talk about how you met. What first attracted you to each other?

4. Remember a time of grace, a time you felt God present, in your marriage. What led to it? What changed because of it?

5. What can you ditch from your "covered wagon" to make room for the new life in your relationship?

FOUR

"I Never Said That!"

Communication &
Conflict Resolution

Jesus said to them, "A sower went out to sow. And as he sowed, some seed fell on the path, and the birds came and ate it up.... Other seed fell into good soil and brought forth grain, growing up and increasing and yielding thirty and sixty and a hundredfold." And he said, "Let anyone with ears to hear listen!"

—Mark 4:1–20

Our canoe ride did not happen overnight. In fact we were married a long time before we learned it is easier to paddle in the same direction. It took years of growing, listening, failing, and trying again to enter each other's worlds. And our canoe ride doesn't happen every day. Some days we are not even willing to get in the boat.

Jesus told the crowd about a sower who went out to sow, and the seed ended up everywhere but where it belonged, except for a few seeds. I think life is a lot like that. You only get it exactly right once in a while. Jesus said about the crowd, "They look but they do not see, and hear but do not listen or understand." He said this to his disciples, who apparently did not see or listen or understand either, because he had to explain the parable, tell three more parables, explain one of those three, and then tell another. Then he asked his friends if they understood. He loved them enough to take the time to be understood. Do we take that time with each other?

Listening and understanding is hard work. It involves a level of investment of self and of self-knowledge that often eludes me. Each of us first learned how to listen in our home, and if our example was not useful, the work of listening is even harder. Neither Neil nor I were very good at communicating in the beginning of our marriage. We loved each other, but we had a hard time sharing how we felt about issues in our lives, or discussing differences with any compassion for the other's point of view. It was easier to stay busy and avoid conflict. When we were married eleven years, Neil was in his thirties and working hard to be successful in his career. I was attending school, working part-time in our State Representative's office as her assistant, and trying to be mother-of-the-year. It left little time for Neil, but I was sure he would understand. This lifestyle, of course, didn't work, and we realized we needed help. I remember saying to a good friend that I knew every opinion Neil had about any given subject, but I didn't know how he felt about anything. Neil simply wanted some of my time and didn't know how to ask me.

We called our pastor, only to find out he was in Hawaii for two weeks. We had friends, however, who introduced us to Fr. Pat Brennan. After he counseled us for a couple of months, Fr. Brennan said, "You're nice people. Why don't you tell each other that." It was good advice. Strange that we had forgotten how! He also recommended that we go on a Marriage Encounter weekend, and that was the best advice of all.

I still don't know exactly what happened to us that weekend, but nothing has been the same since. Described as a "crash course in communication," the weekend gave us tools to use as we learned more and more about each other. I learned how to share my feelings and not to judge Neil's feelings. We began tentatively. On the first evening of that weekend we were asked to write to each other about why we had come. I wrote a flowery load of garbage that I was sure would set Neil straight. He wrote that I had been trying to change him for eleven years, and he was who he was and thought as he did and wouldn't change. After reading his words I said, "Why don't we go home." He answered that he had paid a deposit, and he wasn't going to waste it. Not a very auspicious beginning! But for some reason we persisted, and we began to listen to the couples and priest sharing their stories. What we heard gave us the courage to begin to honestly share our own stories with each other. It was a remarkable time.

A lot happened to us on that Marriage Encounter weekend. We experienced grace, peace, and joy. It was a powerful call to change and to grow, and we decided that we wanted to share this with other couples, and began to give weekends. Doing this, of course, required that we write talks. One of the first talks we were required to write as a team couple was called "Listening." After lots of help from a workshop couple, and after several major revisions, we thought we had it. However, I did think that Neil's part about how he listened could use just a little work. So (trying to be helpful) while I was typing the talk, I added a few lines about how he really listened. Imagine my surprise when I discovered that he was not at all grateful for the improvements I had made! I learned a lot, in the sharing time after that talk, about how I listen.

Patterns of listening

I listen with an ear to find the weak point in an argument. I listen so that I can correct mistakes. I listen so that I can let others know what I know. These characteristics keep me from learning very much about others. If I want to know Neil better, I have to let go of some expectations that I have for the conversation. If I ask him how he feels about something one of our sons has done, it is important to let him tell me and not tell him how he should feel. It is hard for me to simply listen. Other people listen with their motor running...so anxious to get in their point they fail to hear anyone else's. Conversation ends up being something like that game we played as kids called "Telephone," with the message garbled at the end. And nearly everyone has had the kind of conversation at a party in which the person he is talking with is looking over his shoulder at someone on the other side of the room. When that happens to me, I not only feel unimportant, but I realize that talking to that person is a waste of time. Some people have selective hearing. My father didn't always hear my mother when she was trying to explain how she felt, but managed to hear a whisper that dinner was ready. Poor listening and communicating lead to hot denials like, "I never said that," and its counterpoint, "You never told me that." Taking time to listen well can eliminate a lot of this misunderstanding.

Many people honestly believe they can do two things at once and still listen well. When I would talk to Neil at work, I frequently heard the adding machine crunching away in the background. I would feel hurt and resentful that he couldn't make time just to talk to me. Of course this didn't apply to me when I would talk to his mother and do the dishes at the same time. I was very busy, and it was more efficient to do two things at once. One day she told me she felt hurt and resentful that the water was always running when she spoke to me. It surprised me to see the double standard I had about whose time was more important. It is essential that I spend time trying to discover my listening patterns. Unless I understand what I do, I am not able to change.

In order to be fertile soil, I have to be open to change. When Jesus tells of the birds who ate the seed, I think of all the good intentions I've had that have never materialized. I really intended to make a meal for that new mother, and I meant to send a little gift to thank our friends for a weekend we spent with them. I really wanted to make those phone calls, or type the minutes of the meeting, but those seeds never even hit the ground before they were swallowed up by my lack of follow-through.

My rocky ground comes when I have an insight into myself or make a decision to change my behavior but fall back to the way things were. Every time I see an "infomercial" on television about an exercise program, I swear to stick to it this time. I get out the dumbbells and go to it for two or three days, and then the seeds are scorched for lack of roots. Every person has his or her own special kind of thorns. Addictions, overwork, laziness, bad attitude, even a poor self-image can strangle our ability to live in relationship with God and others. Pulling out those thorns can hurt, but the work is essential if we are to bring forth life.

I am fertile soil when I hear the Word of God and allow it to take root in my heart. About ten years ago I graduated with a Master of Divinity. We went on vacation right after that, and I ran out on the dock and threw out my arms and said to God, "Okay, Lord, I am ready, tell me what you want me to do." Now I don't claim to hear God speak directly that often, but this time I did. I know it was God because the answer wasn't what I wanted or expected. God said, "Be still." "Oh no, you don't understand, I have been preparing for years for this moment, I did the work, now use me, lead me...." And God again said, "Be still, I'm God, you're not." So I was still. I really appreciate the fact that Neil kept his patience with me, after thousands of dollars of tuition and tons of support. I was still for eight months. They seemed like a lifetime. And then the phone started ringing. People I had never met called and asked me to give talks or do workshops in areas that were new for me. A group of religious women asked me to speak at their assembly, a parish asked me to do their lenten mission. I figured God had sent them, so I said yes. In the two years that followed I had amazing experiences and met wonderful people. All of which prepared me for the work I am doing now at Dominican University. If I listen and allow God to guide me, I become fertile soil, and the seeds can spring up.

There are hundreds of theories about good communication, and as many books about how to listen and respond take up whole shelves in bookstores. Most of these theories have some truth in them, but not one of them works for everybody. This is because communication is not logic; just because A=B and B=C, A doesn't necessarily equal C in communicating. Communication is movement of the heart, and can't be neatly categorized. Listening and sharing is not science either, to be dissected or broken down into steps that have the same outcome every time. Listening is an art, and like all art it takes years of practice and many do-overs to build a portfolio of strong communication. In another place in the gospels, Jesus talked about seeds, and said that unless a seed dies it cannot bring forth life. Sharing life with another person involves the same willingness to die, to give up the hard shell of protection, to yield to fertile soil, so that life can begin anew.

Importance of really listening

Each time Neil and I come together to share, we are in a different place in our lives and in our relationship. So every day we have to begin again to hear and understand each other. If we begin with kindness, it carries our conversation. It is simple but not easy. I remind myself to step outside of my needs and focus on Neil's.

We have a great friend who lives in New Jersey. Because we live far apart, we rely on phone conversations to stay close. When we talk, Maureen asks dozens of questions for practically the entire conversation. She listens to my answers as if they were the most important thing she has ever heard. And she remembers what I have said and mentions it the next time we talk. Sometimes we get to the end of our conversation, and I realize I don't know how her children are, or what is happening in her life, because I did all of the talking. Maureen has the ability to draw anyone into conversation because of the way she inquires and pays attention. I have learned a lot through our friendship, and I became a better listener when I became aware of my own self-absorption. It is painful to look honestly at ourselves, but self-awareness usually is hard.

It is good to remember that our communication needs are different at different times, too. Sometimes I have a real need to share, and sometime Neil's need is greater. We try to consider this in our conversations. Besides, griping is so very satisfying that we have to give each other a chance to do it once in a while. When I have a problem at work, or a class that went badly, it helps when Neil just listens and doesn't try to fix it. Things don't seem quite so bad when someone listens compassionately. And the feeling of really being listened to is incomparable.

The opposite is also true. The most glaring memory I have of being ignored happened one afternoon when I was sitting at the kitchen table crying. I had just had a huge fight with my mother, and I felt helpless, frustrated and very angry. The phone rang, and after my tearful "Hello," a friend asked what the matter was. I began to tell her, and she jumped in with a story about her mother and how difficult she was. I needed her to listen, not tell me a bigger, better story. Instead of receiving the affirmation I needed, I felt overlooked. It is hard for anyone to stay quiet and listen, especially when one has the perfect anecdote or a moral lesson to impart. However, it is essential to let go of agendas when another person's need is greater.

In any marriage, couples make judgments about this all the time, and one decides to listen more fully to the other. If Neil and I don't step back and pay attention, we find ourselves competing about whose day was the hardest. Stopping that cycle requires asking the right questions and paying attention to the answers. If we do that, we have a much better evening.

Two other things that help communication along are timing and phrasing. Timing is critical. If I have something I really need to discuss with Neil, something that is bothering me, or some worry I have, I try not to unload on him when he walks in the door. I may wait until after dinner, when we have time to sit and talk. We tend to have our most meaningful conversations in the early evenings. It doesn't work when I bring up a problem at eleven at night, while

Neil is struggling to stay awake. All of his energy goes into keeping his eyes open and not into listening. The same is true for me in the morning. We have friends who have all the world's problems solved by 7:00 a.m. after they have walked five miles, but this would never work for me. I am still struggling to be coherent at that time of day. Everyone has to pick the time that works best for them.

There are gender issues that relate to timing, too. It is true that any time you make a generalization about men and women, you have to say that it is not all men and not all women, but one generalization I read has some truth. An author said that women only share difficult feelings when they feel safe in a relationship. When things are going really well, they are comfortable with bringing up difficult issues. Men, on the other hand, cannot understand why, just when everything is going well, she has to bring these things up! One adjustment every couple has to make is to find the best time for working through trying situations. Timing. Which leads naturally to "how you say it."

How you say it

It really doesn't matter what I thought I said, it matters what Neil has heard. I might have nailed my side of a dispute, but if Neil heard something different, or if I haven't expressed how I feel about the argument, we are no further along than when we started. We have to keep checking with each other to see if we understood what was said. This is true in other areas of my life as well. Sometimes when I teach, I look out into the room and see eyes glazed over. Perhaps it reflects poor listening skills, or perhaps I am missing the mark completely. I have to think about that. There is a line from an old Simon and Garfunkel song that seems to reflect many of our discussions, "People talking without speaking, people hearing without listening." These words echo Jesus' frustration with his disciples who heard but did not understand. So I try to phrase things so that Neil can hear me. It's the difference between "You never listen to me!" and "When I talk to you about something that is important and you don't listen, I feel really insignificant." If I say it that way, Neil knows more about me, and he is more able to respond. It's worth the effort to try to understand the other, and the effort to make ourselves understood.

A big part of what you say is how you say it. If you have ever been around a couple who constantly criticize each other, you know how uncomfortable it is to be with them. My mother used to say, "You catch more flies with honey than with vinegar." Though I never wanted to catch flies, her point was clear. It is amazing what a little affirmation can do for our relationship. Affirmation requires that I pay attention to the good things Neil does and is, rather than focus on the mistakes. It means that I go out of my way to say and do things that make him feel good.

The daughter of two of our good friends was married recently. Her dad, Mark, offered a toast in which he quoted a column from Ann Landers that had appeared in the paper that morning. It listed fifteen words young husbands ought to use to keep their wives happy: "I love you." "You look great." "Let's eat out." "Can I help?" and "It's my fault."

The fifteen words for wives were: "You're so sexy!" "Dinner is ready." "I hate shopping." "You're a genius!" and "Here's the remote."

Everyone laughed, but his point was a good one. There are things each of us loves to hear, and it's important for the one who loves us most to say them as often as possible. For me it's the question "Have you lost weight?" Nothing spurs me on to skip dessert and exercise more than the thought that someone thinks I look better.

No matter how good anyone becomes at communication, there will still be conflict. In fact, entering into conflict is an act of love. I don't bother arguing with people I don't care about, but I care enough about Neil to risk fighting. In his book *Good Things Happen*, Dick Westley writes about building community. He names four stages of community: Pseudo-Community, where everyone still agrees with each other and conversation is on the surface; Chaos, when conflict enters in; Emptiness, which requires letting go of self for the other; and finally, Community.

Communities that won't risk chaos will never achieve real community. The same is true in marriage. Unless I am willing to risk chaos, to share my pain or uncertainty with Neil, and unless both of us are willing to empty ourselves and hear the other, we will never be one.

Remembering your story

One thing that helps me listen to Neil when we are fighting is to remember his story. In our years together, I have learned a great deal about Neil, his family, the things that hurt or helped him as he grew up. Remembering these things makes it easier to know what is behind the things he says and does. I know, for instance, that his dad would stop speaking to his mom when he was angry, and those silences lasted a long time. Neil has the same tendency to withdraw, but I have learned how to encourage him to enter into discussion, even into arguments, for the sake of our relationship. I can remember when we were first married and would have a fight. Neil would leave the room and ignore what I was trying to say. I had seen the hurt this caused his mom, and I wasn't going to have this be a part of our relationship. I would follow Neil from room to room, until I finally made him fight. We were very bad at fighting at first, but we learned with practice. I have become gentler, and Neil has learned not to disengage. We think that is great progress! Today, when we work with engaged couples who tell us they never fight, we always ask them if they would like to learn how...and we tell them our story.

I know certain things about my behavior when I am angry. I know what my boundaries are, what I will not stand for, where I am willing to compromise. If I can trust Neil enough to tell him what is going on inside me, we have a healthier relationship. Neil can teach me those things about himself when we can discuss the feelings that he has. And sometimes the feeling isn't about the issue at hand but is a remnant of something that happened years ago.

I remember when our two older boys were becoming teenagers, Neil was often very frustrated over things they did. Now any parent of teenagers can tell you that this is perfectly normal, but Neil's feeling came at times when they actually were behaving well. We spent a lot of time talking about what was going on and why he might feel that way. We talked about needs, like loving and belonging, which he might have. And we were able to understand that what was going on wasn't between Neil and our sons but Neil and his dad.

When Neil was just starting high school, his dad was transferred out of state and decided not to move the family. From that time on his dad commuted on weekends. So, for many of the important moments of Neil's adolescent life his dad wasn't there. We talked about this for a long time. I was able to share with Neil how good he was as a father, and that the boys could always rely on him. It was surprising to Neil that something that happened so long ago could still stir up feelings and conflict. Talking about it helped to resolve that conflict.

Whatever you read about conflict, you'll find that conflict is an essential part of relationship. In fact there is an estimate that about sixty percent of our interaction with people involves spoken or unspoken conflict. So when I hear couples say they never fight, I wonder how that can be. Conflict allows us to know each other better. We have had to learn to fight well, and to take care of each other while we do. For healthy conflict we need guidelines and skills which include consideration, the ability to express ourselves and be accepted, and the ability to move toward resolution.

To be considerate in a conflict requires discipline and a core of caring for each other. It is important to avoid belittling or sarcastic language, to give equal time for sharing, to avoid criticism or blaming. Doing these things helps create a safe space where honest sharing can take place. I have stopped Neil in his tracks with a well-timed reminder of a past failure or with a sharp comment meant to prove I'm right. He has expressed frustration that I can out-argue him. When I do these things, I don't win—we both lose.

Self-expression involves some understanding of our own feelings and an ability to articulate the problem clearly without going off on tangents. I am very tangential and find it difficult to stick to the topic and be specific. Yet when I can do this and be honest with Neil, we are able to resolve our conflict more easily.

One of the rules for fighting we learned in Marriage Encounter was to hold hands while we argue. It does sound strange, but we have found over the years that staying physically close while we argue helps remind us that our relationship is more important than anything we disagree about.

Keeping conflict healthy

Resolving conflict calls for change. One problem in resolving many conflicts is that often there isn't a clear case of one side being right and the other wrong. Often conflict arises over style. One person likes a thing one way, and the other another way. Neither one is right or wrong. Neil played basketball in college and still enjoys sports a great deal. My preference for entertainment includes going to the theater, listening to music, and going to lectures. One solution to the conflict this might cause is to simply do things separately, and sometimes we do. But we also have a desire to do things together, and have had to compromise and explore the alternatives to just "being at odds." Without keeping score, we try to balance our outings to include both of our interests. By doing so we have become more interested in each other's preferences and have made our conflicts much healthier.

One conflict we faced early in our marriage was raised by my opinion that Neil spent too much time watching sports on television. He came by this honestly, as his father not only watched one game on TV but listened to another on the radio at the same time. We talked about how important it was to him to watch sports. I listened to his desire to have me watch with him sometimes. I said it was frustrating, and I felt shut out when he could be so absorbed in a game that he did not notice what was happening in the house or what I was saying. He listened.

Neil agreed that some games were not that important, and I agreed that some games were. What happens now is that Neil usually turns on a game toward the end, and I often come and watch. For us this was a loaded issue, and in order to be rational about it we had to set aside a time to talk about it, try not to get angry, and stay calm. Because we focused on positive ways to work it out, and supported each other's viewpoint, we have learned to enjoy something together that once was a point of separation.

I am sometimes carefree with money, and this leads to conflict in our relationship. I tend to stuff change into my purse or pockets, and am always pleasantly surprised when I find a five or ten in an outfit I haven't worn in a while. Neil handles money in business and likes to keep paper money in order, tens, fives, and ones facing the same direction. He is a Certified Public Accountant, and order and balance is a high value. He has passed some of this on to at least two of our sons. Once when Paul was seven, we were driving to the city. I asked him to get toll money out, and he said, "Mommy, your wallet is a mess." I was amazed to watch him take my money and arrange it not only by denomination but so the bills faced the same direction. I knew I was hopelessly outnumbered.

Fortunately I am not extravagant, which helps a lot, but I often don't take the time or have the interest to be helpful to Neil. One thing I do that really bothers Neil is I that buy groceries "creatively." I don't always make a list, and I don't often check the cabinets to see if we have any of the things I am buying. I know I have gone too far when I open the pantry door and see three bottles of catsup in a row on the shelf, staring at me. Neil doesn't have to say anything; his arrangement of the bottles is indictment enough. But it is important to talk about it. I sense the anger Neil feels, but I need to listen to him. I need to talk about ways I can be more careful, allow him to express what my carelessness does to him, and then I need to change. If I am wrong, saying I am sorry is only a beginning. My behavior is a better indication of my being sorry than just the words. Conflict resolution should lead to action.

I think one of the main reasons people avoid conflict—at least one of the reasons I avoid it—is that if we truly listen to another person in a conflict, we will be changed. Loving another person, however, means that we will be open to that change.

Reflection questions

1. What makes it hard for you to listen to the other person? What can you do to improve?

2. What does conflict in your relationship feel like? Has there been a time when it has been painful? Have you been able to heal that?

3. Loving another asks you to be willing to enter into healthy conflict. How have you come to know each other better through conflict?

4. How has listening to God in your relationship caused you to change?

FIVE

Two in One Flesh

Sexual Intimacy

Then the Lord God said, "It is not good that the man should be alone; I will make him a helper as his partner."... Therefore a man leaves his father and his mother and clings to his wife, and they become one flesh.

—Genesis 2:18–25

The first time I met Peter's mother, I knew I wanted to be like her when I grew up. Peter was Neil's best friend in college, and his mother came to visit one weekend. She was smart and funny, gracious and lovely, and her slow Southern drawl didn't hurt. You could tell she enjoyed young people, and could stay up late.... These qualities help when relating to college kids. Over the years

Neil and I have visited Mida when we were in New Orleans, and she seems to improve with age. We recently talked to Peter, and he shared a story about his parents, now eighty-four and eighty-one, which told me she is still my role model.

It seems that last year Peter's dad had a little prostate trouble. Not unusual for a man of his age, but it did require surgery. When he came out to the waiting room and told Mida, she asked, "Did you inquire if this will affect our sex life?" When he answered no, she said, "Well, you go right back in and ask the doctor." Albro stood at the door of the doctor's office and cleared his throat, "Mida says to ask you if this will affect our sex life." A startled doctor apologized for making assumptions, for not mentioning anything about this. When asked how often they had relations, Albro answered, "One or two times a month." The doctor assured Albro that there should be no problem, recovery time was about three weeks, and things could get back to normal. A relieved Albro faced his wife in the waiting room. "What did he say?" she asked. When Mida heard Albro's answer, she reached into her purse and pulled out a calendar. "See," she said as she pointed, "There's a star on last Sunday night, and Wednesday, and this week, see there's a star on Monday and Friday. Why Albro! We make love two times a week, not once or twice a month." All the time she was speaking, his eyes were getting bigger. He barely breathed, "You put stars on the calendar?!" His face glowed with a very proud smile.

Fortunately, the surgery turned out well and nothing has changed. Well, one thing. Albro used to ask, "Do you want to spend some time together?" Now he simply says, "Do you want to put another star on the calendar?"

"....and the two become one body."

I still want to be like her when I grow up!

Mida and Albro are real. I couldn't make a story like that up! They did not get to this place easily. It takes a long time to become that comfortable with each other. Trust builds with each encounter, and sometimes trust is destroyed and needs to be built again. Studies by sociologists tell us that sexual relations in marriage are more fulfilling and exciting than in other relationships, but at the same time there are comedians who joke about how boring and rare sex is in marriage. There is truth in both of these theories. Because sex is another form of communication, it requires the same care and effort that verbal communication does. Sexual intimacy is both a symbol and the cause of the union of man and woman. We are sexual beings every minute of our lives. What distinguishes married love from every other human relationship is that it is an exclusive and lifelong union of husband and wife. Marriage provides an opportunity for oneness that is unique among all relationships.

In a pastoral letter to his people, Archbishop Hunthausen writes: "Sexual love is therefore a constitutive part of matrimonial spirituality, not something secondary or accidental." The Song of Songs celebrates the passion and love of a man and woman, with language that is earthy and fresh. Filled with passion, the lovers in this poem are completely focused on the other. He says, "How beautiful you are, how pleasing, my love, my delight…" She answers, "I belong to my lover and for me he yearns."

This utter absorption in the other melds two persons into one flesh. It took a while for Neil and me to come to this kind of self-giving, this lack of inhibition. I loved him so much, and both of us thought sex would be something we just knew how to do. And sometimes that was true, but other times making love was nice but more trouble than it was worth. There were times in our marriage when sex was difficult and confusing. We have had lots of stages and changes in that part of our relationship, and Neil and I have grown and changed. Because sex is another form of communication, there is always something new to learn. Unlike romance novels and movies, a man and a woman usually don't start out as experts in this area.

One of the reasons Neil and I got married was so that we could have sex, all the time, no fears, no guilt. Not the most edifying reason but probably one of the top ten for people our age and older. June used to be the month with the most weddings, with June brides setting the standard. I believe that was because nobody wanted to wait another minute after graduation to have sex. I learned recently that September and October are now the most popular months. I am not surprised. Times have changed. And in our case our experience was limited to each other, so neither of us had a great repertoire to fall back on.

I had heard horror stories of how much sex would hurt, and how it was really only for men, that women just went through the motions. My most interesting recollection is the nun in my high school who encouraged premarital chastity for us with these words, "Sex is evil, sex is dirty, save it for the one you love." Contrast that with the swirl of information from Masters and Johnson, and the misinformation from authors like "J" that bombarded us in the sexual liberation during the 60's and 70's when we got married, and it is a wonder any of us survived.

Much more than instinct

Woefully under-informed, Neil and I soon discovered there was a lot more to sex than instinct. Sex relies on a lot more than our bodies and wanting to make love. Our psyches and feelings are all tied up in that part of our relationship. Often my own feelings of inadequacy get in the way of my enjoying sex. When I am self-conscious, focusing on my body, my weight, my veins, my performance, then I lose sight of Neil. Lovemaking is "other" centered.

As much as I love Neil, sometimes in the middle of lovemaking I would remember the time a park ranger caught us making out in the woods. Although we weren't doing anything really wrong, things the man said had made me feel ashamed. Later on those memories returned unbidden, and I felt the same shame. Then I would feel guilty because that memory spoiled our time together.

Not only are there visual memories that affect our relationship, but for people who have suffered sexual abuse, there is physical memory. Sometimes problems are deeper than just silly remembrances, and couples need to seek counseling to help work through past experiences. It is important to know that healing is possible with the right help.

It's interesting how critical Neil and I were of our sexual performance in the beginning. There were so many things to concentrate on. Timing was tricky, variety seemed important. Armed with manuals and game plans, we sometimes took ourselves so seriously that we forgot to laugh when we made a mistake.

Few guys admit to doubt in areas of sex, so Neil's friends were unreliable sources of information for him. None of my friends talked about sex either, and a gynecologist I went to dismissed my questions abruptly. So if ever I was unable to respond, I judged I wasn't much of a woman. Not one of our four parents had ever admitted to having sex, let alone given us any pointers. And neither Neil nor I were good at sharing our doubts and feelings, and so it took a while for our understanding to catch up to our desires.

Other things accompany us to the bedroom too, like the kind of day it has been and how we feel about ourselves. There have been times I have stopped Neil mid-move because I didn't think he had talked to me enough before he started making love. Or Neil might be less loving if I had forgotten the laundry in the dryer. Lovemaking and scorekeeping do not go together. If I feel neglected or taken advantage of, it is hard to respond to Neil at all.

We have learned that lovemaking at night begins at breakfast. The kind of affection we share, the compliments we give, the laughter and the listening, all help to create desire. It's hard to feel sexy when we haven't even spoken to each other because I was on the phone all evening or Neil was watching a game. All of these factors can determine whether we say yes or no to each other, or how much of ourselves we are willing to give.

It helps to think about being romantic, but of course that means discovering what the other thinks is romantic! For the longest time I tried to romance Neil with notes tucked into his briefcase or in his suitcase, and with thoughtful little gifts given for no special reason, because those are the things I find romantic. I was hurt when Neil said how silly he felt when a heart dropped out of his papers in a meeting. He, on the other hand, found it very romantic to grab me and ravish me on the couch, something he wished I would do. We have learned that it is better if he writes the notes and I throw him on the couch. When we take this time, we are drawn more deeply into the mystery of our relationship. There is a Sufi tradition that says, "You think because you understand one that you understand two, because one and one are two. But you must understand the 'and.'" The "and" is the mystery that draws us together. The "and" is unique and particular to each couple; it is the piece that makes the whole relationship possible.

Another part of our journey influenced Neil's and my sexual relationship significantly. For the first eight years of marriage we experienced infertility. We belonged to the generation that actually wanted to get pregnant on the honeymoon. (In fact, a year after our honeymoon we received a Christmas card from Caren and Tom, a couple whom we had met in Bermuda. They signed their names and the names of the twins who had been conceived in the first month of their marriage.) As the months went by after our nuptials, we became more and more anxious. After a few years we began infertility testing. First Neil had to spend a painless but humiliating afternoon at a clinic—and then the tests for me began in earnest. In addition I had to take my temperature every morning, and we had instructions about when, how, and in what position to make love. To complicate things, Neil was traveling on business at this time, and I would be desolate when he would be away at the "perfect time."

Even more painful than the tests was the disappointment each month when I would start my period. I would cry alone in the bathroom but would try not to upset Neil. He didn't want to make me feel bad, so we just kept our feelings to ourselves. Infertility can cause doubts about one's sexuality, and although we didn't talk about it, our sadness was always just below the surface. We became reserved with one another.

We never had to deal with an unwanted pregnancy, but I know that friends who are super-fertile have just the opposite problem we did. Every time they make love, in the back of their minds is the question whether they will then have another child. All of these things are hard to talk about.

"Pass the catsup"

The greatest boost we had in our sexual relationship happened about twenty years ago, when we were married about thirteen years. We had worked through lots of things, had two sons and a really solid marriage, and we were invited to attend a workshop on sexuality. My first thought was, "Don't rock the boat." But my second thought was more useful. "If I can get rid of one inhibition, it will be worth the cost of the day." It was! The most important thing we learned was from a little pantomime skit the presenting couple did. It seems she had prepared a wonderful steak dinner which she was enjoying thoroughly, but which he wasn't eating. She speculated to herself that perhaps his steak wasn't properly cooked, he fumed because she should know he liked catsup with his steak. She said to herself how sad she felt that he wouldn't eat, and he got his back up and refused to eat the steak because she wouldn't pass the catsup. Neither one told the other what they were thinking; they simply made judgments and grew more and more isolated. The moral of the story, of course, is to ask for the catsup to be passed. Tell each other what delights you. Don't try to guess, ask! And don't expect your partner to read your mind. It is simple advice but really profound. It opened up a whole new way of being for Neil and me, and we continue to find ways to ask and tell.

As we grow older our relationship continues to amaze and delight us. There is a familiarity and ease that comes with middle age that is better than all the young adult angst and high excitement. Passion is deeper and bonds are stronger. I do believe that this came about because we have been willing to address the needs and frustrations, feelings and judgments that have come up in our marriage. Sexual intimacy is more than just physical sex; it is being able to hold one another when sex is not possible, like after having a baby or following surgery.

And it includes small touches, holding hands on a walk, eyes lighting up when we meet. At night we read the paper in bed, and

Neil tickles my back while we do. While they were young, our boys often came in to chat at this time, and I think they enjoy seeing us physically close. We once heard a talk by Fr. Chuck Gallagher who started Marriage Encounter. He said that everything in our children's world was telling them that sex outside of marriage was great. We were the only ones who could tell them how wonderful sex is *in* marriage. He challenged us to try. I hope we have done that for them.

The human touch has the power to heal and is really important for physical health. The power of touch to heal became evident again months later when we received the early morning call that my father had died. Neil instinctively reached for me and held me. His arms were passionate and comforting, and he gave me the strength to deal with the next few days.

I believe that is what it means in Genesis to become one body. We leave our families and cling to each other. We are naked and have no shame. God's desire for us is that we be passionate about God, about life, and about each other.

And don't forget the stars in the calendar!

Reflection questions

1. What models of marital sexuality did you see when you were growing up?

2. Lovemaking is centered on the other. How are you self-giving in your sexual relationship?

3. How does your passion for each other reflect God's passion for us?

SIX

Knowing and Being Known

Intimacy in Relationship

Jacob was left alone; and a man wrestled with him until daybreak. When the man saw that he did not prevail against Jacob, he struck him on the hip socket.... Then the man said, "You shall no longer be called Jacob, but Israel, for you have striven with God and with humans, and have prevailed."

—Genesis 32:23–31

Intimacy is elusive. It is hard to put into words the oneness that real intimacy brings. When Jesus wanted to remain with us after his death, he gave us his body and blood so that he could be present to us for all time. Intimacy is not so much about location, it is more

67

about connection. And so we celebrate our intimacy with the living God in the sacrament of Eucharist. When Tad Guzie speaks of this sacrament in his book *Jesus and the Eucharist*, his words are simple. "The real Jesus took real bread and wine and identified himself with it." I find these words very solid, and they speak to me of a union that other definitions do not. To be identified with Jesus, to be taken in the reality of life as we are, is the nature of sacrament. In marriages the real Jesus takes the real elements of our lives, takes real men and women in their glory and in their weakness, and identifies himself with us. We are not asked to be other than we are, but by the act of his identifying with us, we become other.

Grace enables us to be other, that is, more than we could be alone. It is a great mystery that a man and woman become one. The intention of sacramental marriage is more than just human commitment, and our understanding of the grace of this sacrament is gradual. I have very strong memories of our wedding day: I awoke and realized it had finally come. All the planning, all the work, were focused on us becoming one. Neil and I were young, twenty-two and twenty-one, and although we were in love, we did not fully understand the promises we were about to make. Our understanding of marriage was romantic, but the future was unknown. I was aware of happiness, exhilaration, slight panic, and a sense of deep joy.

Someone once said that a wedding has less to do with a marriage than the fact that whenever you begin a difficult journey it is good to be surrounded by friends and wearing nice clothes. That certainly fit our wedding day. I was really looking forward to celebrating at the reception with our family and friends. Though we vowed to be faithful forever, Neil and I did not really understand the unshakable oneness to which we are called. It wasn't until much later, after years of struggles and joys, of learning who we are and growing into who we could be, after bearing children together and learning to be parents, of failing and then beginning again, that we began to understand the vows we spoke that lovely September day.

There have been volumes written about marital intimacy—with lots of different viewpoints and definitions. But there is some common ground. There is some consensus that becoming intimate involves the areas discussed in earlier chapters like the bringing together of our differences, satisfying communication, healthy conflict, and a strong sexual relationship. But intimacy is different for every couple, and it is purchased at great price.

Barriers to intimacy

In our world today there are several barriers to intimacy, including the emphasis on individualism, a growing cynicism, and changing expectations about marriage. It is hard to let go of an ingrained lifestyle of making decisions for one. There is often a fear of losing self by joining with another. But if we cannot let go of our independence and move toward interdependence, intimacy will remain a dream. One of the courses I teach in college is "Theology of Marriage and Family." I listen to many young people who are skeptical about the possibility of ever having an intimate relationship. Many of them come from families that have been broken, and they are afraid they will experience the same pain they witnessed in their parents. For a few there is almost a cold cynical appraisal about the possibility of really belonging to another, yet there is a great need to belong. These two opposite reactions are in tension. And culturally we expect more from a marital relationship than previous generations did. When marriages were arranged, people did not imagine that their spouse would fulfill all of their dreams. The expectations were more in the area of shared vision and values, and hopefully pleasant companionship. The choosing of a spouse because of strong attraction brings with it a whole set of expectations about needs being met. Often it is difficult to meet those expectations.

But I think a most serious barrier to intimacy is the lack of personal reflection, a kind of examination of conscience, if you will. We are so busy that there is no time to spend thinking about our behavior and its effect on those we love. It takes time to think about what persons or events in our past cause us to be guarded and stingy in our relationships. And sometimes it is painful to bring up those hurts that keep us from loving fully. Yet the heart of marital intimacy is self-knowledge. My capacity for closeness is rooted in my sense of self. The more I understand myself, my strengths and gifts as well as my weaknesses and fears, the better able I am to fully love Neil. He and I have committed to journey together toward becoming whole human beings. We hold each other's stories in our hearts, and we learn from each other how to love. The challenge of intimacy, like the challenge of conflict, is that I will be changed.

In their book *Marrying Well*, Jim and Evelyn Whitehead refer to the story of Jacob wrestling with the angel as a moment of intimacy. That story intrigued me, and I have read it over many times. I have thought of Jacob when Neil and I have wrestled and strained to listen and learn from each other. In the course of the wrestling Jacob is wounded, but he holds on! Later he asks for a blessing and is given a new name, Israel. God came close to Jacob and embraced him. When Neil and I fight, we are in each other's arms the same way, testing, sometimes hurting each other. But we hold on. And in the end, like God and Jacob, we are both different. If we really listen to each other, we reveal ourselves. In the intimacy of the struggle both of us give up something of ourselves for the other.

Neil and I do not fight easily, and so we have to decide to engage in conflict instead of being indifferent or avoiding it. We have friends who fight too much, and they know they need to do less fighting and learn to fight more intimately. Because of the intimate knowledge spouses have of one another, there is the danger of being wounded, but out of that pain we receive a new name, Us.

Remembering each other's stories

It seems there is no easy path to becoming one. It is a path with obstacles and surprises, and the greatest surprise is that in becoming one we also see God face to face. Intimacy asks us to change and grow, to risk and trust. Our love as husband and wife is a sacred trust. It involves work because it centers on understanding—first self and then another person. Intimacy results when two people share this work.

The gift in marriage is a companion to walk with, to share life, to challenge and be challenged by. I can fool other people, but Neil knows me inside out. He knows the things that have hurt me and caused me to be cautious. He knows the things I do well, and he can help me remember them when I forget. Because I know Neil's history, I also know what hurts him, and that carries a responsibility to care for him.

I remember a conversation I had with Neil's mother just after Neil and I started dating. She told me that what she loved best about Neil was that when he hung the laundry outside he did it in order, first sheets and towels, then pants, shirts, underwear, and the socks in pairs! I asked her if that was really what she loved best, and she said it was. I remember my conversation with his mother when I am angry with him for working too hard or stressing out when things don't go perfectly. Because I know this, I am able to help Neil be easier on himself, to relax and enjoy life more. When I remember his story, I don't distance myself when he is distant, but I try to help him see his own goodness. In turn, because Neil recognizes when I feel threatened or insecure, he can explain things to me or just listen to my fears. When we do these things, trust builds between us, and we are better able to risk in the future.

When I think of risk, I can't help thinking of Tobias. The Book of Tobit, in Scripture, is one of my favorite adventure stories, a story of a journey, of Tobias journeying with an angel to be exact. The angel tells him to marry a woman named Sarah, and says, "Do not be afraid, for she was set apart for you before the world existed." Now Tobias had good reason to be afraid. Sarah had been married seven times already, and all seven husbands had died on their wedding night. Even more disconcerting: while he and Sarah were in their wedding bed, the servants were outside digging his grave. What Tobias knew, and what we have learned, is that we are not in this alone. He invited his wife Sarah to pray with him, to ask God to bless their union.

A great mystery in marriage is that in the process of our journey toward one another, in the deepening of our intimacy, we begin to banish evil and to heal the losses and pain in our lives. Together we are invited to find a way to bless these losses and this pain. In Mark's gospel when Jesus was asked to comment on divorce, he spoke, instead, of oneness. He hinted at the mystery God has created in each new couple. Jesus said, "For this reason a man shall leave his father and mother and be joined to his wife, and the two shall become one flesh...so they are no longer two, but one flesh." Jesus spoke of the ideal, that each couple is set apart for each other, like Tobias and Sarah, since before the world was made. It is as if our coming together is part of the dream God has for us. This seems incredible, and it might be true.

Remembering how Neil and I met, and the many events that paved the way for us to meet and fall in love, I believe in my heart that we were meant for each other. We have often wondered about the fact that we came from different places, made choices to go to one school and not another, and ended up sitting at the same table that night. When there are features or news on television that take place in Washington D.C., nine times out of ten there is a picture of the Washington Monument. I always say a prayer of thanks that I saw it shining that January night. I was a bit more lively than any girl Neil had dated. I am eternally grateful to his mother, who never said a word about the fact that when she met me I had on a miniskirt and sported a blond streak that made me look like a skunk. And Neil was so different from any other guy I had dated, so different from me. He had qualities I knew I needed, his sense of organization and structure were traits I desperately needed in my life. And my ability to dream and see the positive in life has given Neil the ability to relax and enjoy life more.

We have different skills in parenting, too. Neil has taught me to value discipline, and I have helped him to see he didn't have to do anything but just be with his sons. Trying to become two in one flesh has taken lots of time and effort and trying things on for size, but the trying has allowed us to live out God's dream for us.

Intimacy, God's dream for marriage

When thinking about dreams it is important to remember that they have two parts, the first part is God's, when God asks "What if...?" The second part is ours, when we respond, "I'll try." I believe that when God sees us, he asks these questions: "What if this man and woman could be two in one flesh? What if they could take a whole bunch of different values and traits and find a new way of being? What if they really knew that they are the image of my love in the world?" Our response lies in the way we have drawn out the best in each other, in the way we have learned to bless the struggles and pain, the joy and fun. Living as two in one flesh is a challenge, and it is a good description of intimacy. Nobody receives a manual telling how to deal with this challenge; understanding what it means to be two in one flesh takes a lifetime. Intimacy involves sharing feelings and emotions, it means being able to be honest and vulnerable, and it requires mutual support. The foundation of self-knowledge is essential because we cannot ask who "we" are until we ask "who am I?"

It is often easier to say what intimacy is not than what it is. It is not the kind of soulless joining espoused by so many sitcoms today. People really want more than that, even when they don't know what they seek. It is not self-indulgent but relies on dying to self and living for another. It is not simply sexual but is intellectual, spiritual, and emotional. When intimacy involves the whole person—body, mind, and spirit—its power spills over and touches the world. Intimacy seems to come in moments, and you know them when they happen, yet they are almost impossible to describe. But experiencing it even for a moment is reason enough to keep working toward oneness. The greatest gift of marriage is the possibility of being known and truly knowing another person. Our covenant is with a lifelong partner, one who knows us fully, who knows when to challenge and when to support us. Living with Neil, hurting and forgiving, getting it right and getting it all wrong, has taught me a lot about God's dream for us. It is a large dream, and we depend on God to journey with us. The story of God's faithfulness in the Scriptures assures me that God will abide with us as we try to respond to the dream.

God's relationship with the people in the Scriptures is an intimate one. Our first glimpse into the kind of intimacy God desires to have with us is the way God walked with Adam and Eve in the garden. Even after they disobeyed, God came looking for them. I believe they betrayed God's trust not so much by eating the fruit but by turning away from each other, by placing blame. That act violated the dream God had of being two in one flesh, and brought pain into the world. Still, our God never gives up on us. Again God broke into history with Abraham and Sarah, establishing a covenant that would bind Yahweh to his people forever. Throughout the long and difficult journey with Israel, God shared their hopes and dreams, and wept with them in exile.

God sent prophets whose role was to call the people to return to the covenant. Hosea was the first prophet to speak of marriage as a symbol of the covenant. Using his broken relationship with his wife, Gomer, Hosea indicated the depth of God's desire to belong to the people. In the Song of Songs, attributed to Solomon, we hear the passion and intimacy that love makes possible, "My lover belongs to me, and I to him." And finally, God again broke into history by becoming one with us in Jesus. Jesus established a new relationship for us with God, not one of fear or distance but one full of the intimacy of "Abba." Jesus tells us that to know him is to know the Father. It is this oneness, this intimate relationship that married couples are called to live and witness to the world. This means that if you know me, you should know Neil because he and I are one.

Reflection questions

1. How has your understanding of the promises made on your wedding day grown?

2. The heart of marital intimacy is self-knowledge. How well do you know yourself? How well do you share yourself?

3. What is the price of being intimate for you?

4. God's dream for you is that you be two in one flesh. How has your response helped to make that dream real?

SEVEN

And Baby Makes Three

Becoming Parents

And Mary said, "My soul magnifies the Lord, and my spirit rejoices in God my Savior, for he has looked with favor on the lowliness of his servant. Surely, from now on all generations will call me blessed."

—Luke 1:46–55

When Mary discovered she was pregnant, she didn't go to the rabbi, or to her parents, or even to Joseph. She went to see her cousin Elizabeth who was also with child. Imagine the joy of their greeting. Two women, both pregnant, filled with wonder at God's blessing, one older and past childbearing years, the other a virgin pondering the events of the past month.

I have been to baby showers, and I have been large with child. Most of any mother's thoughts and dreams are focused on the baby. In Luke's gospel we are told of Mary's canticle or song. The words she sings are the birth song for Jesus. I imagine she crooned them to him after his birth when she nursed him in the night. And she probably taught them to Joseph.

I know of a village in Africa where birth songs are central in a person's life. When a woman plans to become pregnant, she goes away from the village to a quiet place, and she sits and waits until a song comes to her. She returns home and sings that song while she and her husband make love. As the birth of her child nears, she teaches the song to the midwives, and they sing it for her during labor when she cannot sing. When the child marries, the songs of both the bride and groom are sung. And when it is time to die, the people gather and sing the song of the dying person to carry them into the next life.

One of the courses I teach is a Service Learning course, "Religion and Culture: Native American Spirituality." The students and I study throughout the semester, and then we take a two-week camping trip to South Dakota and Montana and spend time with the people of the First Nations. Once when we were visiting the Crow people, we celebrated Eucharist with them. At the end of Mass the priest asked the women to sing for us in the Crow language. They sang several hymns, and taught us the chorus of one we were familiar with. When they were finished, one woman began to sing alone. Her voice was full of passion and pain. It reminded me of family, of intimacy, and of death. I found myself crying. Afterwards I asked her about the song. Her brother had died during the last month, and just before his death, his daughter came to be with him. She had been away from the reservation for many years. Somehow she remembered his song, one he had kept all his life and which she had heard as a child. She sang it over and over to him during his last days. The words, the melody brought him great peace. The woman gave that to us as a gift. I imagine that as Mary stood at the foot of the cross she remembered those words sung in joy years before, and she asked God to remember his mercy.

Our culture doesn't give such gifts. We do not have a community that is as constant, and we live lives that are isolated and ritually poor. Many of us were not sung well into our own lives, and we don't know how to begin the song. If this is true, we have to learn to sing our own birth songs before we can sing to our children. Or we can learn from them.

Sing a new song

There is an old saying that goes, "new house, new baby." We had no idea how true that saying was until 1973. The company Neil worked for in New York had been sold, and we were transferred to California. We were visiting one of the factories before we left and stopped to see the man who had been president of the company. He asked how we felt about the move, and I told him, quite uncharacteristically, that I was sad because we had to cancel our adoption plans and start again in California. He told me that his brother, who was a lawyer, often placed babies and that he would talk to him about us. I thought he was crazy; it takes years to adopt a child.

Two months later, the phone rang as we were packing boxes to move. The call was from the lawyer. Our baby would be born in three weeks, we were told, no problem—go set up our new home, and they would call us. In a state of shock we closed our house, said goodbye to friends, telling practically nobody about the baby because we did not believe it ourselves. We flew to Los Angeles, planning to stay at my cousin Ellie's house until our house was ready. I woke at about 3:00 a.m., unable to sleep. Early that morning I called the lawyer to tell him where we could be reached. He told me the mother had gone into labor at the exact time I had awakened. He would call us later when the baby was born.

Neil and I paced together. Later that morning we found out we had a son, who weighed almost seven pounds and who was waiting for us to come and get him. We named him Peter, and called his grandparents to let them know the news. We called the builders of our home and got an emergency closing, turned on water, electricity, and gas, and went over to clean Peter's room, the bathroom, and the kitchen. Our furniture was somewhere in Nebraska, so we arranged to have it let into the garage while we were gone. We caught a plane and flew back East to meet our son.

We had nothing ready for a baby, no furniture, no clothing, no diapers, and only four days' notice, no time to write a birth song. But we had love. And we had a strange ability to deal with craziness. I thought about Matthew's story of Mary and Joseph and their flight into Egypt. The gospel says that when the angel told Joseph in a dream that Herod wanted to kill Jesus, Joseph and Mary left in haste. Neil and I weren't that holy, we weren't in any danger, and an angel didn't come in a dream, but we certainly could identify with the haste that they had to make! We were scared, beginning our family away from our parents and brothers and sisters, in a new place for us. We had to rely on each other to learn how to be parents. And that wasn't such a bad thing after all.

In a way, adopting a baby starts parents out even. I had no special time to prepare for motherhood, and felt completely helpless when Peter was put into my arms. I remember I had a cold the day we picked him up, and I was so afraid that they might not give us the baby if I coughed, so I tried to sound as if I was burping. On hindsight, that probably sounded worse.

But Neil and I started off on the same foot, sharing the baby, the jobs, and the joy. Peter was an interesting, independent child from the beginning. He took to the world right away and began investigating as soon as he could. That meant getting down from our laps and going off on his own. After waiting six years for a baby I had hoped for more cuddling, but Peter was very busy, and there were things to explore and places to go. Peter was extremely strong-willed and determined. The first time he walked, he got up, walked across the room, turned around, came back, and carefully sat down. We swore he had practiced in his crib. It was Peter who taught us how to sing him into life.

We were so happy being parents, but we also had to adjust to a different way of living. For years we had been able to pick up and go whenever we wanted. We had privacy and a fairly orderly home. Our schedules were built around our needs, and these had to shift drastically with the arrival of a small person. Overnight we found ourselves never having a hot meal, loading our car with baby paraphernalia just to go out for a few hours, muttering about how the pioneers crossed the country in a covered wagon with everything they owned!

Peter really loved Neil, and I found myself feeling left out when they would go off to do projects together. Neil had incredible patience and would always take Peter when he ran errands; they were a team! I sometimes was annoyed that I had to be the disciplinarian and Neil got to have the fun. We had to learn how to share the fun and the work. Neil learned to care more about manners, and I learned to pick up the toys in the driveway before Neil came home.

Shortly after Peter arrived at our home, Neil's cousin Beverly also came to stay. She wanted to go to college in California, and we were so glad to have her live with us. It was the first time I had ever had a sister, and we enjoyed talking, cooking (she was much better at it than I was), taking care of Peter, and just being company for each other. I had wanted to go back to college, too, and so we arranged that she would take classes on Monday, Wednesday, and Friday, and I would take classes on Tuesday and Thursday. It was a wonderful arrangement!

On Peter's first birthday, Neil lost his job. He had been given a great promotion when we came to California, but now we had no connections to obtain another job. It was a difficult time.

Then there were two

And of course, to top it off, after almost eight years of wanting to get pregnant, we did! We were delighted, but it would have been nice to have insurance. The baby was due at the end of February, when Peter would be almost two. We thought that was perfect. Except that Tom decided to come six weeks early, during a slight earthquake, which has proved to be a prophetic sign for him! Neil and I had only begun our Lamaze classes. When we arrived at the hospital, I told the nurse I hadn't finished the course. She told us not to worry, she'd give us a crash course that night. We didn't see her much after that. Babies were being born everywhere, even in the hall. Doctors won't say that earthquakes bring babies, but they all showed up right after that one!

At birth Tom looked great, but a couple of hours later the nurse came to have me sign forms to give him oxygen. I was still euphoric and happily signed without asking what the problem was. When she came back again with a doctor, I began to worry. I asked if I should consider baptizing him. She told me she had done that hours ago. That was when I got scared. Tom had a form of hyaline disease that was very severe. He was transferred to UCLA's neonatal unit, and he spent his first ten days on one hundred percent oxygen and a respirator. It was grace that brought him there because they were researching his particular disease at that hospital. So many babies had been born in Orange County that night that all the neonatal units were full, and we had to send our baby far away. I remember standing alone in the hall as a stranger took the baby away, wondering why I was letting him. Neil had to drive fifty miles to the hospital to be there when Tom arrived. I had never been so alone.

I don't think we could have gotten through that time without Beverly. She took such good care of Peter and made it possible for us to spend time at the hospital with Tom. After a month he was on low oxygen, and the doctor said we could transfer him to a hospital closer to home, as he probably needed another month or two to breathe on his own. They moved him earlier in the day than planned, and I wasn't there. So I asked the nurses to put the phone in the incubator, and I told Tom I was sorry I wasn't there, but I would be at the new hospital when he got there. I told them they were trying him on room air, and if he would just do well on it, he would be able to come home. He never went back on oxygen, and we brought him home three days later.

There were lots of new things about Tom we had not experienced with Peter. For one thing he was in quarantine. We had to keep him away from everyone, especially his brother, because Peter could have germs that would be dangerous for his baby brother. That meant that when I nursed Tom, I had to leave Peter crying in the hall. But Peter was resourceful and quite effective in getting even. Whenever I closed the door, he would flush something I liked down the toilet, like our season's tickets to the symphony or a bottle of Joy perfume. I couldn't be angry because his little heart was breaking.

This time was really hard on Neil and me. For months Tom took a long time to nurse, and ate every two hours around the clock. I have pictures of me during this time, my eyes almost shut with exhaustion. Neil felt helpless with this son because he couldn't feed him. Tom cried a lot, and I was the only one who could comfort him. I was exhausted with the demands he made and with trying to keep up with a two-year-old. We were both very worried about Tom, but neither of us could talk about it. It was as if voicing our concern would make it happen. We were afraid to sing his birth song because his life was so fragile. So we didn't. I felt somehow responsible for seeing that Tom survived. I was afraid all the time and couldn't ask for help. Neil and I went through the motions in our relationship, but it was a time of isolation.

Another move

Seven months after Tom was born, we were transferred again, this time to Chicago.

Because I was nursing a baby who couldn't travel, Neil had bought our house by himself. We chose Arlington Heights because it had a great library, a hospital, and a paramedic unit (the first in the country actually). We knew we would have to take Tom to the emergency room from time to time, and I told Neil I wanted to be able to run through the snow if we had to. I was a little apprehensive letting Neil go alone because he and I care about different things in a house, but he did a great job, and we loved our new home.

As Tom got better, caring for him became easier. However, he had some problems associated with his birth that required extra attention. I threw myself into taking care of him. He was very small; at six months he was only nine pounds because of all the setbacks he had had. Today he is six feet, six inches tall and strong, but back then you'd never have guessed he would grow so well. He had motor problems, large and small, and we were soon doing physical therapy on crawligators at Lutheran General Hospital. He needed speech therapy when he was two, and it is hard now to believe that he was late talking. Peter helped as much as he could. He really liked his little brother and couldn't wait until they could play together. The first time Tom sat by himself, Peter ran upstairs, got his little chair and a bag of old shoes, and sat his brother down to play shoe store. "What type of shoe are you look-ing for?" he asked seriously. Tom was mesmerized and became Peter's faithful sidekick for years.

Tom loved to snuggle and be read to, and he had a very kind heart. He went out of his way to make people happy. When he was four he had surgery, and the surgeon told me that before he went to sleep, Tom told the doctor he knew he would do a good job and not to worry. Tom loved to do projects, especially with his older brother. Anything Peter suggested, they did. They built forts that occupied the entire basement. Once they even nailed the blankets to the walls and furniture. That was not a good day.

We lived through the snow of 1979 when they were six and four—and the boys had a huge snow fort out back, with rugs on the floor and supplies to keep them going. As they got older they constructed some amazing haunted houses, entire Lego cities, and domino set-ups that took five minutes to fall down. Tom still loves to snuggle, only now it is with his wife, Heather. He has always gotten lost in books, is ready for the next project or adventure, and is sharing his enthusiasm with their twin sons, Justen and Mason.

There's a charm

Five years after Tom was born, just when we began to think we wouldn't have any more children, we found out we were pregnant again. We moved Tom and Pete into one room and planned for the new baby. In a very serious conversation Tom told me the names he had decided on for the baby: Suzie, Francie, or Lightning Shock. Fortunately he had forgotten those names by the time Paul was born.

Paul was a happy baby and fun to be around. When we first saw him, we noticed his dimples; he could melt your heart with his smile. To this day is it hard to get mad at Paul, and he knows it! Right from the beginning his brothers took to him. They wanted him to come with them wherever they went, and I had to keep close watch. The Christmas when Paul was two and a half, we went to Marshall Field's in the mall to see the tree and have dinner. I was paying for the dinner, and Pete and Tom kept asking if they could go to the toy department. (You could see the toy department from the restaurant.) The waitress took forever, and they kept nagging, so I finally told them they had to hold onto Paul's hands and only go to the toy department. They promised.

Two minutes later I reached the toy department, and the boys were not there. I searched all around, called the guard, looked over the balcony and saw a choir singing Christmas carols, and thought they might be there. I ran through the crowd frantically but couldn't find them. All kinds of horrible thoughts ran through my mind. I prayed hard, asking God to tell me where they were.

I claim to have heard God speak on rare occasions, and this was one of them. God asked me when I had ever taken the boys to Marshall Field's toy department, and pointed out that we always went to Sears. Sears was at the other end of the mall. I was frightened to leave where I was, and afraid not to.

So I ran over to Sears, and when I got there, I saw the three boys, Paul in the middle, hands firmly held by his brothers, happily looking at the toys. Peter's first words were, "What's the matter Mom, I told you we would watch him." I can't remember ever feeling so grateful.

Paul was interested in everything, and he was very easygoing. When Paul was little, Neil and I were still giving Marriage Encounter weekends. We would take turns with other team couples, taking care of the children whose parents were leading the weekend. One Friday when Paul was three, I was getting ready and he came into our room and asked, "Mama, do I know the people we are staying with?" I told him no, and he asked, "How many nights will I be there?" I said "Two." And he said, "That's three pair of underpants, right?" And then he went and packed his bag.

Paul grew up on soccer fields and basketball courts. In fact I was coaching Tom's soccer team when I was seven months pregnant with Paul, so he began early! Neil coached all three boys in grammar school, which he really enjoyed because he got to spend a lot of time with each of them. Paul didn't have a set schedule because a lot was determined by his brothers' schedules. As we learned to sing to Paul, his brothers helped us with the words.

Of course, Paul was the easiest of all the boys. I have a theory that once your children outnumber you, you relax and enjoy them. That was certainly true with Paul. When I took him for his fourth year check-up, I asked how much he had grown since he was three. The doctor smiled and said, "I don't know, you haven't been here since he was two." I couldn't believe it, and I felt guilty. He said that after all we went through with Tom, we deserved an easy child. Paul was not neglected, but he would be the first to tell you that we never took him to the zoo. Actually we did, we have pictures to prove it. He was in a stroller, however, and might not be expected to remember. We had a similar experience when they reissued the *Star Wars* movies, and Paul told us he had never seen the first ones. We had a family marathon of *Star Wars* movies and enjoyed his reactions!

The advantage to being the youngest is that Paul got to do other things, and to do things much earlier than his brothers. He was a neat little kid to have around, and Peter and Tom used to ask if he could go with them. Occasionally this was a problem, like when we had a blizzard and they taught him to jump off the roof into the snow drifts. But he survived their attention and grew up to be lots of fun. While Pete and Tom were in school, Paul and I got to do lots of art projects and go to museums. He took art lessons and still has a great interest in and flare for it. Paul enjoyed sports and played soccer and basketball. Because of his early exposure with his brothers, he knew a lot about the games when he began.

Paul's greatest gift is his compassion. Even as a little boy he knew when someone was unhappy and would quietly come over. Now a senior in college, he plans to be a psychologist and work with kids.

Celebrating their differences

Nostalgia is a wonderful thing because you only remember the good times. It is important to mention that there were some very hard times with the boys as well. It is not easy to raise children in our culture. There are external distractions and temptations, there is peer pressure and rampant consumerism. And often our greatest strengths become stumbling blocks. Pete's strong will helps him to get things done, but it also made it hard for him to ask for help. Tom's desire to make people happy got him into trouble at times. Paul can care too much about others, at his own expense. Each of us has to learn to find the light and the shadow in ourselves, and to understand that these are two sides of the same coin.

Neil and I have received so many things from our children. Peter taught us how to be parents, and Tom called forth strengths we did not know we had. Paul came to us when we had learned how to share the joys and struggles of parenting, and he completed our family.

What we have learned with our children is that they come with their own way of being. As parents we share our lives and our love, and our most important job is to try to help them to grow into the person God created them to be. Once I was angry with Peter. He had just spent all of his grammar school graduation money on a stereo. I said that he was careless with his money and hadn't saved as I thought he should. I said he did not have good values. His answer was very important. He said, "I have values, Mom, they just aren't your values. And I respect yours." He was right. He has used his talent with machinery and electronic equipment in jobs he had from the time he was fifteen. I don't care for those things, but he does. His talents and gifts are different from mine. I told Peter I was sorry, and that I would try to respect his values. I also added that sometimes he got carried away, and I reserved the right to point out when he did. He said that was fine.

We learned very early that each child is different, with unique gifts and needs. Once when Neil and I were opening the store, we took two vans down to the south side of the city to pick up some shelving. I rode down with Pete and back with Tom. I liked to play games in the car, so I asked Pete to close his eyes and describe a dairy farm. He gave me an "Oh mother" look and said, "Lot of cows, lot of grass." I said that was true, you had both of those on a dairy farm, and changed the subject. Coming home I asked Tom the same question. He closed his eyes and said, "What a beautiful day, the sun is shining, and the cows are in the field. Why are they running? Oh, it is dinner time and they are going back to the barn." He brought them into their stalls, fed and milked them, and the next day two of them won blue ribbons at the state fair. I realized I could never buy these two boys the same books. And Paul is a blend of the two opposites. He also taught us what he needed whenever we listened to his hopes and dreams.

Although an angel didn't come to us in a dream at the beginning of our parenting (as with Mary and Joseph), we discovered that God had placed a different dream in each child. I once heard a tape by Paula Ripple on Eucharist that deeply affected my parenting and my teaching. She reflected that the only difference between her and the homeless people she passes each day on her way to work was that someone had believed in her dream. As parents we can't dream our children's dreams for them, but we can teach them how to discover what their song is. We walk with them and sing of our dreams for them as they grow. Then we let them go so that they can find the path that they were made to follow. And we pray that they will find a community of faith who will sing with them through the joys and triumphs of their lives, as well as in the times of sorrow and loss.

Reflection questions

1. How were you sung into life?

2. Becoming parents leads you into a foreign land. What changes did you (or would you have to) make to go on the journey?

3. Talk about the challenges and gift of each child you have been given.

4. Your children's strengths can be their stumbling blocks. What is required of you as parents to help them navigate through life?

5. How can you nurture the dreams that God has placed in your children's lives?

EIGHT

The Power of Ritual

Doing It Over 'til You Get It Right

They devoted themselves to the apostles' teaching and fellowship, to the breaking of bread and the prayers.

—Acts 2:42–47

Our wedding anniversary coincides with the first weeks of school. And during those weeks every organization, every sports team, and every school activity holds their first parent meetings of the year. On one anniversary we had meetings on the preceding eight evenings. Neil asked where I would like to go to celebrate and I told him I could not face getting one more babysitter, or leaving the boys one more time. He suggested we take them along. Wise man! We went to Benihana, the Japanese-American restaurant where food is prepared at your table with a great flourish. The boys were mesmerized.

On the way home Paul, who was five, asked in his deep voice, "Mama, can we go to that restaurant next year on your wedding anniversary?" I looked at Neil, and he nodded, and I told Paul that sounded like a good idea. He continued, "And every year, on your wedding anniversary, can we go to the same restaurant?" It occurred to me that he was asking for a tradition, a ritual surrounding this occasion, and Neil and I both agreed that it might be a good thing to do. "But not in between," he finished. "I hated the food." The following September 9th, as the five of us walked through the door of Benihana's, Tom, who was now eleven, confided to the hostess, "We come here every year on my parents' anniversary. It's a family tradition."

It is important to ritualize the significant events of our lives. In our Judeo-Christian tradition we have always commemorated God's action in our history. The people of Israel were instructed to tell the story, even after they came into the land. It is expected that children will ask about the ritual because that is what children do. We are then given an opportunity to tell the story. Ritual opens the way for teaching. And so we commemorate important events like anniversaries and birthdays. We don't have to instruct the people at the table how to sing "Happy Birthday" when the lights are dimmed and the cake is brought in. The ritual done every birthday teaches us. Neil and I have glasses that I purchased on our first wedding anniversary. They are old and fragile, and we only use them on anniversaries. We have a toast every year; a couple of times we only used water, and once we forgot but woke up before midnight and went down and toasted. Then we put them away until the next year. We do these things because we were created with a need to express ourselves ritually.

Human beings are hardwired for tradition, for ritual, and children are very in touch with that. Anyone who has ever tried to put a two-year-old to bed can understand the power of ritual. They never get tired of the same story, over and over, and don't you dare change a word! Without the proper number and order of prayers, glasses of water, trips to the bathroom, and kisses, it is impossible to get to sleep. If we think back hard enough, we can remember the words, the gestures we repeated to keep bad things at bay.

When I was little, I was afraid of ghosts. I don't think I had ever seen one, we did not have television, so I must have heard of them somewhere else, and I was sure that a ghost was going to get me! My brother Tom created an elaborate ritual for me that let me sleep peacefully. He would crawl into my room and be the baby "ghoster." He would act silly and make me laugh. The baby was followed by the mother ghost and then the father ghost who in turn told me everything was fine. Then the bad ghost would try to come in, but an arm would reach out, grab him, and pull him away from the lintel of my doorway, and I was safe. This was always followed by a whistle blast. Tom would then tell me the policewoman ghost, who was always on my ceiling watching over me, had captured the bad ghost and taken him away. "She" would whistle a couple of other times in the night, and it let me know I was safe. I didn't need that ritual for long, but while I needed it, it brought me great comfort. I kept that in mind when my own children went through the monster or ghost periods, and tried to help them create ways to be comforted.

Special holiday rituals

Holidays are times when ritual is terribly important. You can understand that best when you try to have a smaller tree one year or skip the lights on the roof at Christmas. I am especially aware of the rituals at Thanksgiving. It was always a great feast when I was growing up. Christmas was at Aunt Lillian and Uncle Jim's house, but we hosted Thanksgiving. Our house would be filled with aunts, uncles, my Nana, and all the cousins. My aunts would each bring part of the dinner, and the platters on the table would be heaped with food. The meal was tradition, unbreakable, down to the last olive and jellied (not whole) cranberry sauce. Nana and Aunt Lillian were the only two who liked turnips, and they exclaimed over how wonderful it was every year.

When Neil and I moved across the country, the hardest part of being so far away was holiday meals. I found myself duplicating the menu my family had for Thanksgiving dinner, but I incorporated whole cranberry sauce (Neil's mom coached me over the phone with the recipe) and black cherry salad, which Neil loved. His cousin Beverly, who was living with us at the time, and I presided over the kitchen that first year in California. I did surprise myself by making turnip. Somehow it made my Nana and my Aunt Lillian feel closer. In fact, I still make turnip every year, though nobody can stand to eat it. I just use a tiny turnip now, but it wouldn't be Thanksgiving without it.

When we moved to Chicago, we were so lucky to find friends who included us in their holiday meals! They became family for us, as we were so far away from our own families. The gift of that gesture was most evident during the Thanksgiving that Paul had a ruptured appendix. I spent almost every day and night at the hospital for nine days, coming home to shower and then go back.

Everyone else came and went, and Neil spent a couple of nights with him. In the middle of all that was the Thanksgiving feast. Our dear friends Bob and Mary Ann invited our whole family, including Neil's mom, to share their meal. I will never forget how grateful we were and how good that turkey tasted.

When I ask my students to think of a family tradition, they often speak of meals and particularly Thanksgiving, with big steaming casseroles of lasagna, hand-rolled tamales, proper New England turkey and stuffing. Their descriptions tell me more about their families and their lives than any other thing they share. For one thing people tend to sit in the same place, their place. Long after the meal you can close your eyes and see the table and where each person is seated. If someone in the family dies during the year, the seating can feel awkward on the next holiday. At a family meal conversation is ritualized, moving from the exchange of pleasantries to recalling memories. When I was little, my cousins and I would leave the table as soon as we could after eating. But when the crème de menthe was served, we would sneak back in to listen. That was when the good stories were told.

My students have told stories of similar memories. What amazes me, however, is that so often these holiday meals are the only ones families share. Sitting down every night for the family dinner isn't all that common anymore. Jobs, sports, and privacy have replaced the gathering as a priority. The sharing of the day's events, of things that happened with friends, of just being together, doesn't happen all that often for many families.

When Neil and I married and had children, we had to figure out how we would eat together. I no longer put mayonnaise in a crystal dish, but I always had a tablecloth or placemats, and flowers and candles. We set aside dinnertime as a special time to share our day and our thoughts. We have always begun the meal by holding hands and saying grace. Because we started before they were born, the boys joined right in, and they took turns leading grace. The only exception was what we called a "restaurant rule." When we ate out, we would still say grace but wouldn't hold hands. Fair enough! Another rule—ours—came when they were older: no twisting arms during prayer.

It was fairly easy to plan dinner when the boys were small, but as they grew up and got into sports and went to work, it took a lot of creativity to keep that time sacred. We had a very flexible dinner hour, anywhere from 5:30 p.m. to 9:00 p.m. There were times when it was just impossible for all of us to be there, but if a couple of days had gone by, I would serve fondue when we were all together. They loved it, and it took at least an hour to eat as we had to cook each piece of meat. Later on when Pete and Tom were away at college, our table was quieter, but it sure was easier to coordinate three schedules instead of five! Now that Neil and I are alone, it would be easy to let some of the rituals slide, but we don't. Rituals help us find meaning, and it is important to set aside some sacred time each day just for us, to fuss a little over it, and to share our day with each other.

Other family rituals take place around holidays. I always thought it was very wise of the people who set up the church year to include Advent and Lent. Those two seasons give us a chance to start fresh with family prayer and ritual. Advent in our home was especially fun. We had a handmade felt Advent calendar, and the boys could take turns putting the symbol onto the cut-out tree. We lit the wreath every evening at dinner and had a time to say a special prayer. I used little daily Advent prayer books because the boys liked being able to read from them instead of having to make up a prayer.

Another thing we did was to set up an empty manger in the front hall, with a basket of straw next to it. All during Advent, if you did a nice thing for someone, you got to put a piece of straw in the manger to make a soft bed for baby Jesus. Friends of ours, Ron and Denise, had the loveliest custom. The first day of Advent they would put all of the crèche figures out at the farthest points of the house, the wise men and camels to the east, and the shepherds to the west. Mary and Joseph were north, but Jesus was hidden. Each day their children would move the figures closer and closer to the empty stable, until finally on Christmas, everyone arrived. As families trim the tree, or sing favorite carols, they are drawn closer by the power of ritual.

We have fewer family traditions surrounding Lent until Holy Week, but the season always gives us a chance to think about our lives and to have times of shared prayer. It is a more serious time; we celebrate Eucharist during the week more often and work on areas of our lives in which we would like to do better. Holy Week each year provides rituals that are timeless, and we are challenged and strengthened by participating in them. This is because there is power in ritual to transform our lives. I have heard it said that Jesus only gave one "liturgy talk": "The Sabbath was made for humans, not humans for the Sabbath." Liturgy is the language the church uses to try to touch the place in the heart where people can be transformed. When it becomes too rigid or too perfunctory, it misses the mark. When it resonates, everything is possible.

After the resurrection the disciples noticed that often when they were sharing a meal, Jesus was there. And they began having meals together hoping that he would come. That is what we still do. The ritual enables the reality, and expresses, in a tremendously powerful way, the presence of God. Annie Dillard says it best when talking about the guitar Mass she attends, that if we really understood what we are asking, the ushers would issue life vests and we would lash ourselves to the pews. I love that mental image, and just thinking of it has carried me through many a tepid liturgy.

Symbols carry life

More important than music and rubric is the way the primal symbols are used in our prayer. Water, fire, oil, bread and wine, the Bible, the cross, footwashing, and the laying on of hands have been symbols of our faith for 2,000 years. They were chosen because each in its own way draws us into the mystery who is Jesus. Each symbol has its light and darkness. We hear in the Easter Vigil readings that water brings life and death. We are soothed, refreshed, sustained by water. Jesus called himself Living Water, and we are born into the community of faith through the waters of baptism. Our liturgy and our lavish use of water combine to transform not just the person being baptized but the entire people who witness it. Each moment of our lives is marked by these nine symbols, from the moment we are born until we die. The funeral liturgy enables us to find meaning in the loss we have experienced. Different stages of our lives are marked by fire, oil, bread and wine. We learn of our faith in Scripture, and we fashion our lives in the way of the cross. Our rituals continue to connect us to all those people who have gone before us and all who will come. In Christ Jesus we are one.

There is a book, *The Circle of Life*, that is filled with pictures of ceremonies from all over the world, celebrating birth, death, puberty, and marriage. All cultures have had ceremonies for these events in the community, but some cultures have done them better than others. There is a ritual in the mountains of Italy celebrating the passing of a boy into manhood. One of our sons was intrigued by a picture showing a boy being passed naked through a split tree from his mother to his father. The family then binds up the split in the tree, and the tree belongs to the young man for his lifetime. On a particularly bad week in eighth grade my son quietly said to me, "Mom, I think we need to find me a tree." I know that he was asking for a meaningful ritual, something that would hold all of what he was experiencing as a boy becoming a man, and more. Neil and I tried to use moments in our sons' lives that were important. As each one was confirmed, we had a dinner before the ceremony with his sponsor and family. We would read a blessing for a son as we laid our hands on our son's head. It was our sending rite before he went to the larger faith community to be confirmed. As each son received his driver's license, we also blessed him and the car he drove. These blessings gave solemnity to the events, and helped Neil and me to let go of the boys at different steps in their lives.

Ritual draws you deeper into reality and helps give meaning to that reality. Without it we are impoverished. Our culture is ritual-poor. One of my theories is that because we do not celebrate the move into adulthood well, young people seek gangs, which are highly ritualized and use a lot of symbolism. In the absence of good ritual, young people can be drawn to bad ritual. The cruelest thing we did to the Native Americans was not the taking of their land, as awful as that was, but the taking away of their rituals. Children were taken from their homes and sent to boarding schools where they were punished for speaking their language or practicing their rituals. And yet it is language and ritual that define a people. As an immigrant people in this country, many of us left ritual and symbol behind. There is a kind of "beigeness" to our culture because it is devoid of a common thread of ritual. We come from so many places on the globe that it is probably impossible to have a universal set of symbols and rituals, but it is possible for families, communities, even parishes to use symbol well so that we can be transformed.

Reflection questions

1. How do you celebrate your anniversaries?

2. What family rituals were important to you as a child?

3. How have you blended those rituals in your marriage?

4. What new rituals have you created for your family? What would you like to add?

NINE

Healing and Wholeness

Forgive Us Our Trespasses

"And forgive us our debts, as we also have forgiven our debtors...."
For if you forgive others their trespasses, your heavenly Father will
also forgive you; but if you do not forgive others, neither will your
Father forgive your trespasses.

—Matthew 6:9–15

A friend of mine, Judy Logue, says that the concept of "forgive and
forget" comes from chivalry, not from Scripture. She once described
forgiveness this way: "You know you have forgiven when you can
remember the incident but not relive the feelings." I would add one
more piece to her definition: you have forgiven when you are able

to bless the incident. It is easy to bless the good things in life, but when I remember the times I have been hurt and am able to see the blessing that came from it, I know that I have been healed. This may seem to be a contradiction, but it is not. Neil and I have seen the blessing our struggles in early marriage have been to other couples. We were first helped by other couples' stories, and we also know that our story has been gift to others.

I am adopted. I've always known this and have always been comfortable with it, and was so happy that we were able to adopt our son Pete. Often people would ask me if I had ever looked for my parents. I would answer smugly that I knew where they were, I had grown up with them. I also would comment that people who searched for their identity in others were looking in the wrong place. I still think that is true, but there was more to that truth. When I was younger, I was also afraid in some way to find my birth mother for fear she would ask me if she had done the best thing for me. I hadn't come to peace with my parents and didn't know how I would answer that question. I can honestly say now I could answer "Yes," that I had the life God intended me to have. I have always been grateful that she had loved me enough to give birth to me, to have me baptized, and to let me go. I could thank her for that. In my life with my family I learned the things I needed to learn, and they were gift. These things I have understood because in my lifetime I have given and received forgiveness.

One of the best parts about being forgiven is the freedom it brings. Jesus taught us to ask for forgiveness when he taught us how to pray, "Forgive us our trespasses as we forgive those who trespass against us." We invite God to forgive us as we forgive. My teacher and friend John Buscemi told me that this part of the prayer can be understood in several ways. One is the traditional way with trespasses and forgiving. Another interpretation could be, "Lighten our load of secret debts as we relieve others of their need to pay." This would be a way of celebrating jubilee, the tradition in Israel where all debts are forgiven every fifty years.

The Catholic Church has recently celebrated a year of jubilee. When we were discussing that with our son Paul, he said it would be a great idea if all the nations of the world could simply forgive debts and start over. I think he is right. The load we carry when we are indebted can be crushing, and the notion of having debt relieved is enticing. But my favorite way of understanding the prayer is "Loose the cords of mistakes binding us as we have released the strands we hold of others' guilt." Forgiving is making a decision in favor of the other person, over and against their past. It is allowing another to be free to grow and change, rather than holding them fast with sins of the past. We are held hostage as long as others refuse to make that decision, and we can bind others.

I know of a freeing story. A church in Evanston had suffered a tragedy. One of the young men in their parish shot and killed another. The pastor, with great courage, said to the people gathered for Sunday liturgy that this terrible thing had happened to "two of our children." He then asked, "How are we as a parish going to support the two families?" The parish responded in amazing ways, but the greatest witness was the forgiveness offered by the mother of the boy who was killed. She visited her son's killer in prison and told him that fate had made him her son now, and she would walk with him. I do not know if I could ever forgive the way that mother did. And her strength was nurtured in a parish community that understood and worked toward reconciliation.

I have always loved the part in the story of the raising of Lazarus—after Jesus calls Lazarus out of the tomb—when Jesus turns to the community and tells them to unbind him. It is in my primary community, the relationship I have with Neil, that I became unbound. Because we are committed to continue to loose the cords that hold us, to let go of the expectations we have of each other and which keep us bound, Neil and I are able to share that gift with our community as well.

Being bound up

Looking back on the beginning of our marriage and the people we were then, it is not surprising that we ran into difficulty. But at the time I couldn't understand what was happening. If I could put a name to the feeling at that time, it would be bewilderment! One reason I married Neil was because I didn't want to marry someone like my dad, whose job was the most important thing to him. Neil "played" basketball for Georgetown, so I knew overwork would-n't be a problem for us. In fact, I thought anyone who played for four or five hours a day would be a lot of fun to be with for life. I never equated his playing with the fact that he was earning his college scholarship. I just saw him happily running up and down the court during games. It was a tremendous surprise when Neil transferred his discipline in sports to a full-blown work ethic when he went to work for Price Waterhouse. I looked forward to going to the park, on spur-of-the-moment trips on weekends. What hap-pened was that Neil had to work a lot of Saturdays. I dreamed of intimate suppers by candlelight listening to music. Our reality was tray tables in front of Johnny Carson!

Neither of us had grown up in homes where feelings were freely shared, and I had no idea how to let Neil know what I felt; in fact, I couldn't even tell myself. I grew farther and farther away from him, protecting my raw feelings with distance. And to really protect myself, I stopped loving him. I wanted to leave him but I was too scared, so I picked fights, threw tantrums, cried, in general acted like a spoiled brat. I made his life miserable. Even though I knew what I was doing was wrong, I couldn't seem to stop. And everything I did made me more aware of how awful I was. One evening while I was crying about something, I asked, "Why do you put up with this? Why don't you just leave me?" Neil took my arms and said, "Don't you know you are worth waiting for?"

I didn't know. I didn't even think that was possible. But Neil seemed to think so, and somewhere deep inside me I felt hope, tiny and delicate, about the size of an eyelash, but definitely hope. And hope, once the cords are loosed, will grow. Neil gave me the gift of forgiveness with those words, and with that gift I could begin to forgive myself. It was a gift that took many years to unwrap. In fact, I know I am still unwrapping because when I am down on myself that spoiled brat seems very present! The nature of gift is that we become able to share it with others.

Our son Tom was a bit rebellious as a teenager. He was always a wonderful person, but he made some bad choices, and we all had a rough couple of years. One day he yelled at me, "Why do you and Dad put up with me? Why don't you throw me out?" I heard my own voice in his words, and I heard Neil's in my response. I said, "Don't you know you are worth waiting for?" The gift had come full circle. The gift Neil had given to me years before became a life-giving moment for my son and me. When we are forgiven and healed, we are able to see our true selves, the beloved of God, and because we know it we can share it.

Being forgiven

Sometimes it is good to reflect on the enormity of being forgiven. Because of Jesus we don't have to save ourselves, it is already done. Dietrich Bonhoeffer tells us that the Savior restored the whole world by reconciling everyone with God. Jesus is the one through whom reconciliation is accomplished, and our call as disciples is to continue to extend that reconciliation to others. In marriage God's forgiveness for the people is reflected in the way a husband and wife reconcile their differences, forgive hurts, and heal each other. On the other hand, our willingness to help each other heal gives witness to God's desire for reconciliation. When Neil and I choose to live this way, we not only move toward being whole in our relationship, we give our children hope that they will be able to reconcile as well.

Three years ago our two oldest boys married, and they with their wives are beginning their own journeys toward healing and wholeness in their lives. I have often joked that I didn't ever want to be a perfect parent, I wanted to leave our sons just enough to gripe about at cocktail parties or with a counselor. I know I have given them more than enough. I also know they will forgive me because they know that they have been loved. It is hard to let go of them and yet gratifying to see them looking to their wives for the forgiveness and healing we used to be able to provide. Neil and I are reconciling that in our hearts, too. Our youngest son, Paul, is a senior in college. His level of honesty is challenging to me. He reflects on his life and asks for help to change. He witnesses to us and we to him in an enduring way. Because of the things that Neil and I encountered along our road together, I have learned to forgive myself, my parents, uncontrolled events, God, and our children, as well as Neil. I don't always succeed, but I succeed more often than not.

Learning to be open with Neil gave me strength to work on things I had not even admitted to myself. I spent several years in spiritual direction with an incredible woman, Sr. Irene Dugan. I had long been aware of the effect my mother's mental illness had on me, how her poor health had been so central in my family of origin. I had, however, a much more difficult time acknowledging the effect my father's drinking had on all of us. In some ways I idolized my father, and tended to excuse him more than I did my mother. Even after he died, I had not really allowed myself to be angry with him for not being more involved in my life, or for embarrassing me because of his alcoholism. Sr. Irene addressed this in one of our meetings and asked me when I was going to admit he had been cruel. My immediate reaction was anger. I think I even sputtered. She quietly asked me when I was going to allow him to be human. I left her room vowing I would never return.

It took me several days to even mention the conversation to Neil. When I did, he asked me what I thought. Well, I had been thinking of nothing else for the whole week, but I still didn't know what I thought. Neil helped me sort it out. I finally let myself experience the strong feelings I had stuffed inside for so long. Refusing to heal or to reflect does not change anything, except that it makes forgiveness all the more difficult. Talking with Neil about all of this helped me move to a new level of acceptance and gave me the ability to forgive my father. I really needed the safety Neil provided to be able to come to peace. My father had always seemed larger than life to me. My mother had even referred to him as P.M., perfect man. Now I think she was being sarcastic, but back then I thought it was true. It was hard to think of him as flawed. Sr. Irene's challenge and caring and Neil's support helped me become more honest with myself. In the end I was able to love my father in a new way and to be healed of hurts he had caused. And I was able to go back to see Sr. Irene!

The grace of healing

One of the graces intrinsic to marriage is the grace of healing. We each bring our histories—healed or broken, reflected upon or repressed—to our life together. Our vocation is to help each other become fully human. This means finding a way to share hurts, to risk allowing the other person to know us so intimately that we are willing to open old wounds and allow God to heal them. Marriage, at its best, creates a safe space where this kind of healing can take place. Neil is a person who worries. Sometimes his worry wakes him in the night. When that happens I am able to place my hand on him, on his head or chest, and pray. I ask God to bring peace, I ask for healing for the hurts or trouble Neil is experiencing, and I wait quietly with Neil for sleep to come. I believe that we are supposed to pray together for healing. I feel God's presence when we share our deepest hurts and pray for healing. We are a means of grace for each other, and it is most tangible when we hold one another. Jesus was always touching in order to heal. Lepers were cleansed, ears were unstopped, tongues loosened, eyes opened through his healing touch. The woman with a flow of blood and the villagers at Gennesaret were healed simply by touching his garment. I imagine the women bent over, who for eighteen years had not been able to stand up. The cords that held her bent were severed by the touch of Jesus, and she was free. Jesus' compassion, his impulse to lay hands on her, brought about her healing.

There is healing in human touch. Experts tell us that children who are not held fail to thrive. I believe that is also true for adults.

We need to be connected to other persons to be healthy. I remember a time when we were visiting my mother and father and went to church with them on Sunday. Now their church was not as lively as ours, and there wasn't much interaction in the assembly. But Tom, who was only seven at the time, didn't notice. At the Our Father he reached out his hand as usual and took the hand of the young woman next to him. She began to cry, but he did not let go. After Mass she came to us and apologized. She said that her husband had died at the age of thirty-eight just seven months ago. She said that in those seven months, Tom was the first person who had touched her. The tears were tears of relief because when he took her hand she had discovered she was still there.

Others have touched our lives and helped us to heal as well. Right after Neil's dad died, we were at Mass. The choir was singing "Be Not Afraid" as we walked to receive the Eucharist. We passed our very good friends, Mike and Aggie, who were singing the words, "Know that I am with you through it all." Aggie says she had a strong inclination to just touch Neil on the shoulder. Neil said that when she did that, he felt enormous comfort and he cried. It was the first time he had been able to cry since his dad had died. Our instincts tell us to reach out for others, and when we listen to them it is good.

Forgiveness and reconciliation only happen after truly grieving our losses. An important part of Jesus' ministry was to cure the physically impaired and to heal the brokenhearted. Our love for each other can ripple out to continue to be a means of that healing.

Several years ago I wrote a long letter to my father and mother. Though they were both dead, the writing was a healing time for me. I forgave them things I had held closed in my heart, and I asked forgiveness for things they never even knew I had done.

Forgiving does not say it was alright to have done something, and it doesn't take away any of the consequences. Forgiving simply extends God's mercy. As followers of Jesus we participate in reconciling the world, and it begins with ourselves. So I told the truth, which included the easy and the hard things in my life. Our memories are always a little distorted, seen through lenses that are smoky, smudged, or even cracked. You only have to talk to two or three siblings about an important event in their family to know that we all interpret life differently! But in this letter I was free to speak the truth. I included some of the things I have written about in this book that hurt me, but I also told the rest of the story. There is light and shadow in all of our lives. I think that real healing comes when we are able to hold the light and the shadow together, and realize they are the same.

Reflection questions

1. Forgiving is making a decision for the emerging person, over and against their past. How have you made a decision for the other in your relationship?

2. Psychologists tell us we marry someone who will help us work out the things of our childhood. Has that been true in your relationship? How?

3. There is a grace of healing in the sacrament of matrimony. When have you experienced it? How has it helped you grow?

4. Tell a story of forgiveness in your life.

TEN

Spirituality in Marriage

This is Holy Ground

The Lord said to Abraham, "This is my covenant with you: You shall be the ancestor of a multitude of nations...." God [further] said to Abraham "As for Sarai your wife, you shall not call her Sarai, but Sarah shall be her name. I will bless her, and moreover I will give you a son by her."

—Genesis 17

About ten years ago Neil and I had to give a talk on the Spirituality of Marriage and Family. We spent hours one evening trying to define spirituality for ourselves, and then make it apply to marriage. We had a lot of false starts because all of our training told us

112

that the spiritual life was pious, relegated to monasteries, filled with regular prayer and contemplation, anything but the busy, cram-filled life we led. Instead of our day being broken into periods for prayer, I felt lucky to find five minutes to pray in the shower.

At the end of that evening we had lots of empty pages and nothing written, and we were getting pretty frustrated. Our son Pete came into the dining room, where Neil was pacing and I was wringing my hands over the word processor. He noticed our Bible, and picked it up very excitedly and started flipping through the pages. He started to tell us what "Bro," his religion teacher, had told them in class. Neil and I looked at each other thinking that if he kept going, we'd never get finished with this talk. And then we both realized, this was a sixteen-year-old wanting to tell us about Scripture. I turned off the word processor, Neil sat down, and we listened to Peter's excitement. I remember thinking that this might be the only time Peter would want to talk with us about the meaning of the Scriptures, and it was. I am grateful we did not miss it. We never wrote another word that night, but we went to bed knowing what family spirituality was.

Spirituality is the quality, the capacity to be human. It is being open to receiving and transmitting the life of God, and integral to spirituality is the capacity for relationship. The development of spirituality deals with the person as a whole, and it involves the whole life experience of the individual and the community in which they live.

A married couple has an opportunity to transmit the life of God, together with their children and with the community of faith. This new understanding of the role of spouses has been developing since the Second Vatican Council, when the bishops reaffirmed the necessity of matrimony and conjugal love for procreation but expanded the teaching to affirm the involvement of the whole person in the love between spouses, including sexual love. That involvement of the whole person means that marriage and family spirituality is a daily "living for each other." It involves setting aside our agenda for another's and listening in a way that is life-giving. It means forgiving when it is difficult and seeking reconciliation even when it hurts our pride. Our spiritual exercise calls us to life in the present moment. In families we are open to receiving and transmitting the life of God in the way we share, sacrifice, forgive, celebrate, and walk with each other. Our spirituality is enfleshed in the sacrifices we make for each other. God is seen when we wipe tears, listen to music together, make Halloween costumes, cut a rose and bring it inside with love, hold hands for grace, or make Christmas cookies with the children. Sometimes this daily living is frustrating, sometimes it is routine and boring, but the stuff of our lives is where our spirituality is lived out. Bishop Morneau of Green Bay once said that all of the spiritual life can be summed up in two words, "Stay Awake." In family life we are asked to stay awake to each other's longings and dreams, to stay awake to fears whispered on pillows and to stories told at the dinner table. As we stay awake, our capacity for God deepens.

Sign of the incarnation

As married persons grow and develop, they can help each other become open to God and can be a sign of God's love to each other and to the world. It is essential that couples understand God's place in their relationships. There is an old saying, "Every good marriage takes three." Couples who invite God to be part of their lives, their decision-making, their joys and struggles, find their marriages growing stronger as a result. God is felt, God is made real, in the way they listen, desire the good for each other, and support and forgive one another. Neil and I need to reflect more often on the wonder of this. In his writings, Karl Rahner suggests that "Marriage is a unique sign of the incarnation, of the mystery that the transcendent reality of God became flesh in the person and life of Christ, just as men and women incarnate their transforming reality of divine grace in their total love for one another."

We are graced people.

We are a sign of the incarnation precisely because, in our sacramental way of living, the reality of divine grace is expressed in our love. I remember explanations of grace from the Baltimore Catechism that involved half-empty and full milk bottles, but that never made much sense to me. Actually, I have always understood grace through my relationships. Perhaps it was her name, but my primary and most lasting understanding of grace came from my aunt.

Aunt Grace was a carefree, loving, generous, and slightly ditzy woman, who arrived every Easter at our home with two shopping bags filled to the brim with Schrafft's candy. I remember pressing my nose to the window, watching eagerly for her arrival. She would step out of the car and onto our driveway, white wispy hair trying to escape from under the most outlandish flowered bonnet, and with a smile and a twinkle in her eyes, bearing such abundance that no one could possible eat up all the candy she brought. I always imagined God to be such a gift-bearer, bringing an abundance of grace freely given, with a great chuckle, as we reach for shopping bags with wide eyes and grateful hearts. I know that God has been that gift-bearer in our marriage, bringing abundance especially in times when we needed God's love most. And God invites us to be part of this gift giving, in a particular way through our marriage.

Hospitality, the sharing of love

Neil and I once listened to a tape by Henri Nouwen on the spirituality of marriage. He states eloquently that the charism of marriage is hospitality, creating a hospitable space where others can feel at home. His words remind me of a love story—an epic love story—with all of the grandeur, pain, and ecstasy of *Gone with the Wind*. It is a story of a close relationship between a husband and wife, called to serve together and to dream together. Imagine Sarah to be the grandmother on *The Golden Girls*, and Abraham might look a little like George Burns in *Oh God!* Not your average beautiful couple, but beautiful nonetheless. Both of them are essential for the story because both of them said yes to the journey God had in mind for them. Sarah and Abraham were both witnesses to the covenant, which is God's dream for all people. The promise to Abraham was that he would be father of kings and Sarah would be the mother of nations. The promise to us is that we will participate in the bringing forth of new life as well through our relationship. And, as for Sarah and Abraham, living as sign calls us to serve. Covenant is about service or, as Nouwen says, creating hospitable space. The couple provided a little water in the desert, to wash the feet of the visitors. This is the work of the servant. Our marriage can be water in the desert to others, in the way we welcome them, in the way we serve them. We use our own gifts and experience to be that water. Because Neil and I have experienced challenges in our own marriage, we have a gift to give to engaged and married couples in our ministry. Our credential for doing this is that we tell our story. Every married couple has to discover their own essential part in creating hospitable space for others. The telling of stories, the sharing of lives, is the way hospitality is shared.

Both Sarah and Abraham prepared and served a meal for the visitors. Our marriage is also food in the desert, when we set a place at the table for our children's friends, or bring food to a family who has suffered a loss. Our marriage is food for others when we open ourselves to bringing God's love. Because Sarah fed the strangers, the Lord kept his promise to her. Sarah the realist could not believe what she had heard, that in her advanced age she would become a mother. She named her son Isaac, which means "she laughed." I think of Sarah's carrying Isaac not only as a real pregnancy, but as Sarah and Abraham's willingness to bring forth new life. We also participate in bringing new life when we allow God to dream with us. And I remind myself that there are always two parts to God's dreams. In the first part God is saying, "What if?" The second part is our response, "I'll try." Like Sarah, often we are the last persons we would expect to do such things.

Saying yes to God's dream

Almost nineteen years ago we were transferred to New York. Neil was offered a wonderful promotion and a large salary increase, but it meant a lot of travel for Neil and leaving our home and our community. We decided not to go. We prayed for wisdom, discerned with our friends, and Neil went on several interviews, all of which promised travel and future transfers. One night at about 3:00 a.m., Neil woke me up and asked me if I would like to start a Christian bookstore. I said, "Sure," and he went back to sleep. I was really excited. By the time Neil woke up I had lists of books and gifts and a rough draft of a floor plan. The incredible part of this is that neither of us had ever worked in retail, we had never discussed opening a business of any kind, and Neil had never even been in a Christian bookstore. I did all the book shopping for our family.

Against all reason and with faith in our dream, we opened Earthen Vessels in just a little over five months. During that time we had everything we needed. One evening I mentioned to Neil that I had never read a book specifically on prayer. The phone rang, and it was a sister we knew who told us she had just put together a list of books on prayer. She asked if we would like it. Friends by the dozens helped us to paint, lay flooring, set up shelving, put tags on books and gifts, and even build an ark for the children's section. Neil and I learned about the work as we went along.

Finally the night before we opened, we put the last book on the shelf, looked around, and cried. We were happy, scared, and quite overwhelmed at what we had gotten ourselves into. The drive home was very quiet. As we turned onto our street, we saw that our trees were festooned with toilet paper as if for the heroes of Homecoming. There was a huge sign stretching across our garage that read, "Neil and Kathy are Special Lovers!" And on our front stoop was a bottle of champagne and some body massage cream. We woke up the boys and brought them outside to see what our friends had done. We went to bed at peace, surrounded by all kinds of love. Our discovery that night was that when we dream with God, God takes exquisite care of us.

Action and contemplation

The action part of spirituality is easier for Neil and me than the contemplative part. We seem to be able to say "Yes" to a call. It is harder for us to make time for quiet prayer, and even harder to find a style of praying that is good for both of us. We have always prayed before meals, and when the children were home they took turns saying the blessing. Grace has always had a central place in our meals together. Both Neil and I are people who pray, but we pray differently. I wake in the morning really grateful for the day and for all my blessings. Prayer is natural for me then. Neil is quieter in his prayer, preferring to pray alone, while I like spontaneous, exuberant shared prayer. We decided to try to find a way of praying that both of us would enjoy. After trying lots of different styles and forms of prayer, we discovered that praying with Scripture is best for us. Our story is united with God's story, and when we pray, write, and share our understanding of God's Word, we discover new meaning for our lives.

Often Neil and I choose a passage, sometimes the Sunday gospel and other times a story, such as one of the miracles Jesus performed. After reading the passage several times and discussing our reactions, we formulate a question that relates or applies the reading to our life. Then we write our responses.

Actually our bookstore was the result of one of our responses. The gospel at Mass had been Matthew's story about the rich young man. There is a sadness in the story that caused us to wonder how the young man lived with his decision later. What must it have been like to turn and walk away? What would we have done? We asked the question, "What would I do if Jesus asked that of me?" Then we went to write our responses in the form of a letter to each other. I remember trying to fudge on my answer, wanting so much to be able to say I would sell it all to follow Jesus. But the truth was I could not. I wrote sadly that I would also walk away. Neil and I were surprised to read each other's letters. He had also struggled but had to admit that our possessions were extremely important, he had worked hard to afford our lifestyle, and it would be difficult to leave that behind. We talked for a long time that night about the meaning behind our answers. Our own words convicted us, and we decided to begin slowly to change the way we were living. We looked at our priorities and started to change them. It was a challenge to invite God to lead our journey instead of planning for the future.

The change for Neil was that he needed to let go of control. Since I am the sort of person who doesn't worry too much, I wasn't as bothered by this. But I am also the sort of person who doesn't pay enough attention to financial things. My carelessness had been part of the reason Neil needed to work so hard. I had to change my spending habits completely. Although we worked on these little changes, we were totally unprepared for the surprise God had in store for us. When Neil awoke with the dream of Earthen Vessels, we understood at last the way the Word had burrowed itself into our hearts. We joke now about being careful what you ask of God, but we also know that, during those precarious first months and years we owned the store, we were in God's pocket all the time. And we still are. The store has been successful and has given our family a good living and good friends. It is time now to revisit that passage from Scripture and to ask the question again. And we are trying to gather the courage to do that.

Everyday miracles

Even more powerful than the question about riches were questions we asked about our personal life. Listening to the challenges inside the miracles performed by Jesus led us to miracles in our own marriage. Like Mark's blind man, who was touched by Jesus and saw "people looking like trees and walking," we have experienced stages of seeing the truth of each other and the powerful effect of blindness to each other's need. As Neil and I moved toward wholeness in our lives and looked at the people and the events that shaped us, our own eyes needed to be touched again and again in order for us to see distinctly. The question of "Where am I blind to you?" is still one that helps us to keep the other as our primary focus.

Asking the same kind of questions about the other healing miracles, questions about how we make each other outcast when we consider the healing of the lepers, or about how we need to give thanks, have moved us to change hurtful habits or to become more considerate. The dialogue that brought about the most growth in me, however, was the one concerning the cure of the paralytic in Luke's gospel.

My memory of that day is a clear as my memory of our conversation. I was thirty-six at the time, I even remember what I was wearing. It was a warm Sunday afternoon in spring, and all the boys were off playing somewhere. Neil and I sat in the living room with the windows open for the first time that year, enjoying the breeze and the quiet. As we read the gospel story about the cure of the paralyzed man, we talked a little bit about the kind of day it must have been in the house where Jesus was teaching. The story says that Pharisees and teachers of the law had come from every village of Galilee and Judea and Jerusalem. They, together with Jesus' followers, must have made an immense crowd. The crowd was so large that the friends of the paralyzed man had to climb onto the roof, remove the tiles and lower their friend down to Jesus. When Jesus saw their faith, he said to the paralyzed man, "As for you, your sins are forgiven." Neil and I had intended to ask the question, "Where am I paralyzed with you?"

We never got there. As we prayed over the Scripture, I had a thought. "I would never trust anyone to carry me that way and lower me down." And Neil said, "I know." It was just two words, "I know," but in them I heard all the pain I caused by my inability to ask him to carry me. I had developed a great independence as a child because it was hard to rely on the adults in my life. I would rather have suffered alone than let anyone know what I needed, and that included Neil. I heard and saw all the times he had tried to help me, to give support, and I knew how many times I had rejected that help. I felt a wave of shame as I experienced Neil's hurt whenever my short answer, my shrugging his efforts off had erected a barrier between us. I realized that he was the person God had given me to bring me to Jesus, and that I needed to let him do that in order to be whole. I felt forgiveness, too. Jesus asked the question, "Which is easier to say, 'Your sins are forgiven,' or to say, 'Rise up and walk'?"

One is physical healing, the other spiritual. Neil's faithfulness to me over the years has allowed both things to happen in my life. The question I think of often is, "Which is easier to accept?"

Spirituality is that quality, that capacity to be human—it is being open to receiving and transmitting the life of God. Jesus came so we might have life and have it to the fullest. My mentor and friend Sr. Irene once told me that every person in the world has one vocation, to be fully human. Marriage is the spiritual path God has called Neil and me to follow in order to achieve that vocation. Our main job is to stay awake.

Reflection questions

1. Spirituality is the capacity to be human, and relationship is the place where we become spiritual. How has your relationship shown you the face of God?

2. A charism of marriage is hospitality. How do you share that hospitality in your marriage?

3. Trust is an essential part of relationship and of the spiritual life. How have you grown in your ability to trust?

4. What spiritual practices do you share? What would you like to do differently?

5. How does your partner bring you to Jesus?

ELEVEN

Continuing the Journey

Growing in Wisdom, Age, and Grace

Jesus said, "Everyone then who hears these words of mine and acts on them will be like a wise man who built his house on rock. The rain fell, the floods came, and the winds blew and beat on that house, but it did not fall, because it had been founded on rock."

—Matthew 7:24–27

In Scripture a lot of important things happen on a mountain. The ark came to rest on the mountains of Ararat, where Noah and his family came out and offered a holocaust to the Lord. Abraham was told to sacrifice Isaac on a height in the land of Moriah. Moses came down from the mountain after receiving the law from

Yahweh. And in his ministry Jesus journeyed from the hill country of Galilee to the hill of Calvary to show us how deeply we are loved by God. Along the way he went up another mountain, sat down, and began to teach.

At the end of that lesson he told us about wisdom. The man who built his house on rock had observed the way the world was. He had weathered seasons and knew how to be safe against the elements. The other man Jesus calls foolish. The same seasons, the same conditions attacked his home, but because the foundation was weak, there was ruin. It reminds me of the news reports of great flooding, and the desolation on the faces of the people who had lost everything to the water, the mud, and the debris. Often the houses were built on flood plains, areas that probably should not have been zoned for housing, lots that were chosen more for the view than for practicality. Kind of the way most of us begin marriage.

Each of us comes to our relationships with flaws in the foundation. And it is hard to know why some houses stand while others are washed away. We have all had good friends, the ones with the perfect marriage, everything in the world going well for them. And they are no longer together. Perhaps they did not have enough storms. Or maybe they had too many. I know that in some way it is the rain, the floods, and the buffeting winds that bring wisdom to us. I don't think wisdom comes often to those who have not suffered. It is what you do with the suffering that makes all the difference. A good friend has experienced chronic illness for a number of years. His sight and hearing are diminished, but his sense of humor is not. Bill and his wife Joan continue to share their lives and gifts with others in their parish community, and she has told us that Bill does not complain. Actually, neither does she. They move through days most of us would call difficult with fidelity and inner joy. It is good to be around them.

I have a wonderful student who has had many trials in her life. Illness, the loss of a parent, and a debilitating accident have not dimmed her spirit or her faith. In a paper written for one of my classes she began, "On the whole my life has been wonderful...."

Once when we were giving a Marriage Encounter weekend, one of the couples was dealing with the wife's advanced multiple sclerosis. I watched her husband's tenderness and love in the many things he had to do for her. During a time set aside for sharing, the wife told us that she used to wonder why God had done this to her, why she had to bear so much. She said she had discovered something important. "I am an opportunity for others to be good." These people have built their houses on strong foundations, and they will withstand the storms. My life has been enriched by their example.

Climbing the mountain

These stories are extraordinary, but each of us experiences storms and seasons that can undermine a foundation not built on rock. Once at a party I listened to a friend describe mountain climbing, and my first thought was "never!" I would never put myself in such peril, I would never work that hard at recreation, I would never enjoy that kind of exertion. My second thought was that his description sounded an awful lot like marriage! Mountain climbing is not in my experience so I am probably romanticizing, but as a metaphor for marriage it really seems to fit.

I asked Todd how long it took to get ready for a climb, and he answered that he had been preparing all his life. When you actually begin to scale the mountain, you take a lot with you and the load is very heavy. It gets lighter later on. At base camp everyone is very excited and very afraid. Some people quit at base camp; they cannot let go of their fears and start. The essential part of mountain climbing is that you cannot do it alone, and each climber depends on the others. Trust is terribly important because you are entrusting your life to another's leadership. One person leads one day and another the next. Everyone has different skills that they bring to the climb, and all are necessary. One of the great dangers is a "whiteout," when you can't see anyone or anything at all. During those times you have to believe in the rope that holds you together. Climbing a mountain is slow work, you can't go quickly; on a good day you can do 1,000 feet. It may feel as if you aren't making any headway at all because you have to do something called a "double," where you climb to a certain point and then go back for the rest of your gear.

Always skulking beyond your next move is the danger of avalanche. There are summits, but many climbers are unable to reach them. Todd tried to describe the feeling, his experience of "summiting," and it seemed to be beyond words. All he could say for sure was that God was present. I asked Todd if he had ever wanted to quit, and he answered, "At some points, every single step."

Every married person has wanted to quit at some point. It would be so much easier to stop, leave, and run in the opposite direction than face the changes, dangers, and the need for courage that marriage can require. I once read that at the turn of the century the average length of a marriage was about fourteen years. Death during childbirth was one of the primary reasons, but epidemics, injuries, and simple infections without modern medical treatment or medicines, plus the hazards of nature contributed to the early ending of marriages. My mother's father married three times, spending his season of the twenties and thirties with one woman, his mid-life with a second, and his older years with a third. Statistics today indicate we will have much longer lives, promising that if we stay married we will go through all of the seasons together. As we move through the years, we begin again at each stage like mountain climbers at a new base camp.

The greatest number of divorces takes place in the first two or three years. Base camp is the place where you learn to journey together. Equipment is purchased, packs are crammed full, ropes are checked, climbing strategies are reviewed, and there is great excitement and great fear. It is hard to begin to think of oneself as part of a team instead of as an individual, but that transition is essential or the climb is doomed before it begins. Learning to depend on another, to ask for help and give it, requires setting aside self-absorption and being for others. Each person is called on to bring out the strengths in the team, both on the mountain and in life. Leadership changes frequently. Sometimes I am strong and can lead, other times I need Neil to help me navigate a particularly difficult passage. It was hard to learn to trust enough to do that, but we would not be together if we had not.

Whiteouts happen in a love relationship, too. There are times I cannot even see Neil, or understand what is happening around us. At times when one of us is changing and growing, we have to trust the rope that connects us because it's all we have. Neil has been worried about the store lately. The downtown area of Arlington Heights has been under construction, and our street was often blocked with cranes, moving equipment, and barricades. For two years we didn't know which directions to give to people who called. Business was way down, and we are only now coming out of the slump. And we are lucky; several downtown businesses closed during this time.

When Neil is worried, particularly about finances because this is one of his strengths, it is hard to see each other. He becomes quiet, and I don't know what to say or do to make things better. But we are connected. And we have learned to trust the connection. We have a history of coming through crises. We have private jokes, memories, shared friendship, knowledge of each other when we were young. We know we have been through things like this before and have survived. We have weathered storms and are stronger for them. The hardest part of a new marriage is not having that history, that pattern of response and reconciliation. It is one of the gifts of a long marriage.

A new stage of life
Another gift for us is that our children have grown into wonderful adults, and are beginning to follow their dreams. In June 1998, Tom married Heather. As we sat in the church and watched them begin their life together, I was overwhelmed with gratitude that Neil and I were still together to share the joy. It could have been otherwise. At the reception our youngest son Paul gave a toast filled with humor, love, and insight. Pete and Julie were both in the wedding party, in the midst of preparations for their own wedding in October. I was so full of happiness, all I could do was clutch Neil's hand and accept the handkerchief he offered. Four months later we did it again. This time it was Pete and Julie, changing places in the wedding party with Heather and Tom. Their wedding was completely different and just as special. Our sons found wives who could bring out the best in them. Tom and Heather seemed to know from the start how to be a team. Pete and Julie would have to work harder to get there. I hope that they all find the happiness that God intends for them. It is hard as a

parent to let go of the role of protector and helper and give that over to another. But it is also rewarding to see it happen. Every relationship has roles. I was told that the role of the mother-of-the-groom was to shut up and wear beige, and I believe that the role of parents-in-law is simply to love the persons your children choose. We are learning new roles, being in-laws, and try to listen to what they say they need and want from us.

Paul is nearly finished with college. He has used his college time to learn many things, in particular to gain knowledge about himself. His judgment is good, and he has a great soul. Our greatest wish for Paul is that he, too, finds someone who can help him become the person God intends him to be. Our family is blessed that we live close to each other and can get together often. When Paul is home on break, they all make a point to get together at one of their houses. They are forging friendships with each other that will hopefully support them long after Neil and I are gone. It is relationship that sustains us, and through our relationships we have the potential to become fully human.

Grandparenting is worth waiting for

On March 1, 2000 we were plunged into the newest (and I would have to say the best) phase of our life. The day before, Heather and I had gone out for lunch before her doctor's appointment. She was four weeks away from delivery and quite pregnant with twins. She had to quit her work as a middle school teacher several weeks before, as she was having a little difficulty with the pregnancy. I joked with her that when she went for her appointment, she should tell the doctor she wasn't going home. Actually the doctor told her. Tom was so excited that he e-mailed everyone he knew and called us as he packed her things to take to her to the hospital. Nervous and excited, he asked us to come, and Neil and I decided we would go just for a short time.

When we arrived at the hospital, Heather looked beautiful and Tom's nervousness was gone. They seemed very much able to handle what was happening. We stayed for a little while and then went home to wait for their call and to pray. Justen came first weighing six pounds and fifteen ounces, followed ten minutes later by Mason weighing seven pounds and one ounce. No wonder Heather had been tired. Both babies needed to stay in the special care nursery, and Mason was having difficulty breathing and needed a little oxygen.

As Neil and I returned to the hospital, I was filled with memories of Tom as a newborn struggling to stay alive, hooked up with so many wires. We were greatly relieved to know Mason was not in a lot of trouble, just the usual premie-twin kind of things. We stood at the window of the nursery and watched our son Tom holding his sons, and understood the power of the circle of life. Grandchildren are truly an important reason for being faithful during your children's teenage years. Once they arrive, everything becomes new. As a new dad Tom was comfortable and clearly besotted with love, and the twins were incredible. The nurse asked Tom if he would like to learn how to change a diaper, and he barely breathed, "Can I really?" She hadn't heard that answer before. Heather needed some special care afterward, and because she was on I.V.'s, she could not go to the nursery to see the babies. I remembered how empty my arms had felt when Tom was far away, and I ached for her. But Tom talked the nurses into wheeling Justen down to see her for just a little bit, and it was the best thing he could have done. Both babies recovered quickly. In fact, as soon as Justen was out of trouble they put him in the bed with Mason, and from that minute on Mason improved.

These past sixteen months have been amazing. I didn't know how deeply Neil and I could love. I used to laugh at new grandparents, thinking they certainly exaggerated about how great it was. Actually, they didn't say enough! There is a sweetness and completeness in caring for grandchildren. Heather and Tom have been very generous with the babies, letting us be part of their lives from the first day. I try to watch them one afternoon a week to give Heather some time off. Next year when she goes back to teaching, I will have a whole day with my grandsons. I am looking forward to coloring, reading books, taking walks, and making cookies together.

Heather calls often to tell me about milestones—teeth, steps, words—and it gives me so much joy. I remember with sadness my own mother's lack of enthusiasm when I called to tell her about Peter's first tooth. She said, "Why would you think I would even be slightly interested?" I find I am incredibly interested, and I am sorry for the joy she missed in her life. I also know I am not going to miss it! Neil is a wonderful grandpa, as good with these babies as he was with our own. Once Sr. Irene, my mentor, said of Neil, "He does what love demands." I thought then it was high praise, and I still do. He is still like that. (Tom takes after his father in that respect.) And Neil can't wait to play games, build snow forts, and do projects with the twins and with our future grandchildren.

One of my friends comes from a large family, and her parents have a summer tradition. For one week in July all the grandchildren over ten years of age come to "Camp Hecker" (their last name). The cousins get to spend time with the grandparents, no parents allowed, and they get to know each other well. They come from all over the country, but for that one week they are as close as brothers and sisters. Neil and I are looking forward to "Camp Heskin" one day.

Justen and Mason are teaching us what it means to be grand-parents, just as Pete, Tom, and Paul taught us about parenting. We know the mistakes we made with our sons, and we don't have to make them again. As parents we were sometimes too busy to see the wonder in our children's lives; as grandparents we will not be. We know that the most important gifts we can give are not things but our time and our love. We will try to give fully.

The best is yet to be

Neil and I have been blessed with friends and family, with colleagues and mentors. These people have helped us grow in our marriage, in our spiritual life, and in our role as parents. During times when we were not close, friends have helped us to find each other again. After we had dined with our friend Father Clem one evening, he asked: "How long are you two going to settle for being mediocre with each other?" He told us he had seen us when we were good and wondered what was wrong. It was a long evening, but his challenge and support were the push we needed to grow. We remember being a young couple sitting at the Christian Family Movement meetings, and listening to Bob and Rose Duffy, parents of seven grown children, telling us we would get through the bumps of parenthood. We not only believed them, but we are now the oldest couple in our CFM group. Hopefully we can pass their encouraging words along.

Our studies in ministry showed us how to learn from teachers, some of whom are now great friends. Their wisdom has shaped our life together in many ways. As I pursued graduate studies, I had the feeling that each course came at exactly the right time. Neil told me he felt the same way. We looked for ways to share what we had learned by presenting a workshop, giving a retreat or talk, or working in our ministry with engaged and married couples. Along the way and in the giving, we have learned more about ourselves, our church, our world, and our God. It has all been great gift. The challenge of the learning and of our lives is to find a way to share what we have been given.

We are also finding that the best part of life is now. Something happened to me at fifty. It was as if all my life had been preparing me for this time. Neil would add to that by saying that after fifty, you no longer care so much what others think. It is a great freedom. I think the freedom has come because we were faithful to working through the things that hurt us. There is a saying in gerontology, "What you are at forty, you will be at eighty, only more so." I have thought about that, and it is true. People who are stingy and mean in mid-life tend to become even meaner as they age. People who embrace the world at forty tend to become interesting, wise octogenarians, and others want to be around them. But you have to do your inner work, to look at the light and shadow in life, and bless it. There doesn't seem to be any way around that, only through it.

At fifty-six and fifty-five, Neil and I are a little slower physically, and that will continue to happen more in future years, but we are content. We used to think our parents were odd when they talked about remedies and procedures. They don't seem as odd anymore. We were on vacation this summer, sitting on the deck, watching a boat full of young people water skiing. One young man was crossing back and forth over the wake and jumping high. Neil said, "I could do that once." I asked him if he minded not doing it now. He said, "No, this is best for now." We don't water ski anymore, but we have learned each other's ways, and learned what is important and what is not. Each time of life has its blessings and trials, but I would really have to say that empty nesting is wonderful!

Neil and I still set off on new climbs, taking what we think we need to scale a new mountain, and trying to rely on each other. Sometimes we still encounter whiteouts, and we lose sight of the other, leaving us feeling terribly alone. But it is getting easier to trust the rope that holds us fast, and to secure the pitons that hold our weight. And little things don't seem as critical as they once were. Neil still doesn't like to go out to dinner, and I am getting tired of cooking even though I have always loved it. We have to compromise on that one. It is still hard for Neil to compliment me, but I don't need compliments as much anymore. We do not agree on how the mosquitoes get into the house; I say it is the lights on and the door open; Neil insists there are holes in the screens. I have not turned into the golfer Neil hoped I would be when he gave me clubs for my birthday. But he and Pete play in the church league on Wednesday evenings and have a great time. And I enjoy watching sports on television with him, primarily because I can read, do a crossword puzzle, or draw while we watch. Neil is good company, and I have learned enough about sports to hold my own in a conversation. And both of us love going to the theater. We like different things so we take turns picking the outing.

I still get a little panicked when Neil discusses technical things or finances. A couple of years ago Neil had a rapid heartbeat and had to go to the hospital for a couple of days. When he came home, he sat me down and told me where everything was in his filing system. I was really grateful for the care he has taken of our family. And I have tried to be more of a partner to him in this area. I remembered visiting my father shortly before he died. I wanted him to tell me his deepest feelings, his regrets, the things that were important, and he wanted to talk about money. I said, "Daddy, I don't want to talk about money," and he answered, "I do."

If I had a health problem, I wouldn't go right to the file cabinet or the checkbook, but I have learned that what happens is not always about me. Loving Neil calls me to go beyond my own wants and needs, to recognize when his need is greater and to accept that need, even make it a part of me. It's a lesson that takes a lifetime to learn. We have come to understand that life is not about having everything we want or getting everything right. It is about character and sharing values. We will ultimately be remembered by how well we have loved. All in all, I would say that is great growth; it's not perfect but it works for us. I know that when we finally reach the summit, we will find satisfaction in the effort and love we put into our life together. And through it all we have experienced the presence of God. Sometimes we experienced whiteouts with God, too, but we have learned to trust that the line that connects us will hold. God's grace has brought us this far, and we know it will be there for the rest of our journey.

Reflection questions

1. How have you repaired the flaws in your foundation?

2. What wisdom has come to you from the storms in your life?

3. Marriage, like mountain climbing, is slow work. What is required of you to make the climb successfully?

4. In moments when you have wanted to quit, what kept you from doing so?

5. How have good friends played a role in your relationship?

6. What do you think of when you hear the saying: "What you are at forty, you will be at eighty...only more so"?

7. Where are you in your ascent up the mountain? And how is God present at this part of the journey?

TWELVE

The Paschal Mystery in Marriage

Hidden from Your Eyes

As God's chosen ones, holy and beloved, clothe yourselves with compassion, kindness, humility, meekness, and patience.... Above all, clothe yourselves with love, which binds everything together in perfect harmony.

—Colossians 3:12–14

The crucifixion and resurrection are interdependent. Easter happened because of the crucifixion. Knowing this helps me to recognize that Neil and I, through the stages and events of our life that marked the end of a chapter and the beginning of another, have learned how to "Easter." The first Easter happened to broken, bitter, disillusioned men who had fled to upper rooms or back home

to Galilee, and to shaken, bewildered women who approached a
tomb in deep sorrow. There were no apostles before the resurrection, only disciples whom Jesus had formed in community, carefully teaching them about his Father and his mission. But at the
crucifixion nearly all of them had scattered. Peter denied him, the
rest of the men huddled in fear. The women were faithful but did
not believe. John stood at the cross and then took Mary home.
There was nothing left of the community that had shared the
years, the meals, the stories.

In the midst of that desolation something happened. Nobody
actually witnessed it as it took place. We really do not know what
happened. For some it has become an historic event that took
place 2,000 years ago, for others a stumbling block, and for many
it is the core of their faith. What we as Christians believe is that
Jesus rose from the dead, and we are told that each person who
encountered him was transformed. Each person who met the risen
Lord experienced forgiveness, welcome, and peace. And they
could never see anything the same way after that.

I think we have four different accounts of the resurrection in the
gospels because no two people experience the Lord in same way.
I believe each of us could write a different account as well. After
rising Jesus showed himself as a gardener, a stranger on the road,
a cook on the beach, someone who was willing to deal with our
doubts. He came, and still comes, at all levels of appearance, to
speak to all levels of human need. Many of the visits were in the
context of a meal. And at all of the meals Jesus shared with friends
before and after resurrection, he offered forgiveness. An Easter
insight is that forgiveness is always possible at the gathering.

Easter is more than the vindication of Jesus; it is the process of
conversion for all of the disciples. And so Peter might say that res-

urrection for him meant that John, the beloved disciple, understood and forgave him for denying Jesus. Mary Magdalene would find her voice and would use loving words so that the men could hear her. The disciples on the road would marvel at the removal of their fear and the welcome they experienced when they returned to the community they had fled. Thomas would be grateful that his doubts and fears were respected. And all would be overwhelmed at the experience of love and reconciliation when they encountered the risen Lord.

One of the core beliefs of our faith is that the incarnation is ongoing and the paschal mystery continues to be enacted. God freely chose, out of love, to be bound irrevocably to human mortality so that we can freely choose to accompany Jesus to his passion. Our task as Christians is to discover how to live out this choice. It happens in the daily dying to self, in living out of a concern for another. Marriage is meant to be a distinctive way in which Christians, called through baptism to enter into Christ's death and resurrection, can experience his saving power. We are asked to let go of barriers that keep us from loving, to move from the darkness of sin to the light that is Jesus. This experience encompasses the entirety of marriage, through its passages from early marriage and parenting, to middle years, and finally in the movement toward our own deaths.

At different times in a marriage there is a death of the familiar in order to move to new life. I really believe that Neil and I have had at least four distinct marriages, totally different from the previous but made possible by living and dying to each one. The mystery of death and resurrection contains all of the fear and pain in this movement, as well as the hope that sustains us. Married couples embark on the process of conversion as they are trans-

formed by the experience of death and resurrection in their marriages. If the mystery of marriage is, as St. Paul tells us, revelatory
of the love Jesus has for the church, then that letting go, that
dying, is intrinsic to the bond. The married couple experiences in
their relationship a reality greater than themselves alone, God's
presence. It is a mixed reality, made up of good intentions, missed
opportunities, and keeping faith. Like the disciples we lose our
way, doubt, do not understand, and need forgiveness. When a
married couple accepts the challenge to struggle with these impli-
cations, with this death to self, then God's presence is made
known.

Dying and rising

When Neil and I were married about eleven years, we were in our
thirties and at a point when Neil's career was terribly important to
him. I was very involved in school, work, and activities with the
children. I remember saying to a friend that I had never been so
fulfilled, and I enjoyed hearing her say she didn't know how I handled it all. Life was great until the evening Neil told me he was
leaving me. He was very different that evening, and he meant
what he said. I thought of our early marriage when I had been the
one who had wanted to leave. It seemed only natural that he
would want to get back at me. It wasn't that simple. Somewhere
along the way we had both changed directions and hadn't bothered to tell each other. We were not together, we were traveling
along parallel roads.

I was devastated by Neil's words, and we argued without making any progress. As we lay in the same bed that night, totally separate, I felt abandoned and frightened. I got up to go downstairs,
and unlike times in the past, Neil did not follow me. Sitting alone

in the living room I remembered all the years, the good and bad times, the things we had done together and with our boys—and they were over. Nothing was as I had hoped. It seemed unfair, I was the one being hurt, and I would have to be the one to try to make things right. Neil didn't seem to want to try. I made a decision that I would do whatever it took to rekindle our love.

It wasn't easy because first I had to look at what I had done to cause us to be so distant. I couldn't change how Neil felt, but I could change how I acted. One big area he had talked about was my not taking any interest in his work. I tried to see how my indifference to his job was hurtful. I didn't understand his business so instead of asking Neil questions and listening, I had ignored it. Work was a huge part of Neil's life, and it mattered a great deal to him. I needed to find ways to share that with him.

With a part-time job, two active boys, school, a house, and a husband, I didn't have enough energy for everything. I had thought Neil would understand. He did not, nor should he be expected to—not when he was my last priority. I was able to quit my job, and I graduated from college that year. But beyond the external changes, I changed how I looked at our relationship and tried to put Neil first.

We went to counseling, this time choosing a counselor who supported marriage. Fr. Pat told us we were nice people and asked us to tell each other that once in a while. It sounded pretty basic, but we had forgotten to do that. This period was a time of uncertainty and of waiting. It was a time to learn to love again.

What was grace for us a short time later was a chance to make a Marriage Encounter weekend. I approached it fearfully, thinking it would be awful to spend a weekend finding out Neil didn't love me at all. The opposite happened. We remembered why we had come to love each other in the first place, and we found ways to help that love to grow. On that weekend we forgave each other for past hurts, and I began to forgive myself. We entered into dialogue, a way of sharing feelings and needs that helped us to heal the past, live in the present, and weave a fabric of a future together. We experienced Easter.

The three days

The parallels of the paschal mystery to our own mystery are evocative. The pieces are there over and over in our life, and they call us to be faithful through the pain and to believe in the possibility of joy. We celebrate the Triduum every year to remind us not of a long-ago event, but of a way of living as people of faith. As we enter into the prayer of the church on Holy Thursday, we are reminded of all the table fellowship that has been shared, and we are pointed to the future gathering. Friday plunges us into darkness, and the paradox is that the darkness is the bridge to light. When the burden of pain is no longer possible for Jesus to carry, he cries out, "My God, why have you abandoned me?" This is not despair but the beginning of a psalm, Psalm 22, which ends in these hopeful words: "The generation to come will serve you. The generation will be told of the Lord, that they may proclaim to a people yet unborn the deliverance you have brought." Friday calls us to let go and trust the darkness as Jesus did.

Saturday is the time of waiting, sitting with the mystery. The crisis is past, but the future is still uncertain. Sunday brings wholeness. There is joy and rejoicing, both in encountering Jesus and in the gathering that celebrates that encounter. When we gather in our Sunday celebrations, we bring our experiences of death and resurrection, suffering and joy, our moments of encountering Jesus in each other throughout the week. We gather to celebrate what God has done. At that last supper Jesus showed us how Easter could feel when he washed feet. He showed us that to serve one another, to give of ourselves to one another, is Easter.

And so I believe that footwashing has an important place in building relationships. Important, but so darned awkward! When we make a stab at it on Holy Thursday, it is sometimes contrived and irreverent because it is a pageant, not a part of our lives. There is a stiffness because we do not live the vulnerability of footwashing as a faith community. Nobody ever thinks their feet are attractive. There are all sorts of feet jokes, referring to size, odor, and appearance. Clearly feet are not the inspiration for poets (Carl Sandburg's "little cat feet" excluded). But feet are very important in our tradition. Moses met Yahweh in the burning bush, and Yahweh told him to take off his shoes because the ground where he stood was holy. Not the ground around the bush but the place where Moses spent his days tending goats was the holy ground. Amazing.

Married couples share the holy ground of their daily lives, the places in their homes where they encounter God—sofas, beds, kitchen tables. Places where they are often barefoot and where feet touch holy ground. Only faith allowed Moses to remove his shoes and touch the holy. In marriage our call is to stand barefoot together, so that we can respond to God's call by being vulnerable to each other. Our spirituality is lived out in daily life, and that is our holiness, our holy ground.

We are called to wash one another's feet with the heartfelt compassion, kindness, and humility, the gentleness and patience that Paul speaks of in his letter to the Colossians. The sacrament of matrimony can be a witness to the world of God's love by the way we forgive each other, by the way we hold each other in our hearts. If we are vulnerable, our love for each other will be joyful, and we will give a glimpse of the passion of God's love to everyone we meet.

We are often barefoot in our house. In the early morning my feet can stay toasty warm in bed, or take me to the kitchen to make Neil's coffee. Kindness moves my journey. If a child cries in the night, feet fly barefoot to find out what caused the pain or fear. Heartfelt compassion hasn't time to find slippers. After a crushing fight, lying together separate in the silence of our bed, sometimes a toe sneaks over to ask forgiveness. Stony hearts can hold back, but humble feet seek reconciliation.

There are times when one of us is weak and must be supported by the other. Instinctively we trust the solid foundation of the other. Our life together tells us that we will bear one another up during the times we cannot stand alone. Friends of ours told us that when Roger's mother was dying, Roger's father tenderly washed his wife's feet and dried them with love. The feet of the person he had traveled with during his life were precious to him. Part of the "Yes" we said on our wedding day was that one of us would accompany the other to death. Hearing of the deep love of these parents as death approached has broadened our belief that all of creation is embraced by the resurrection.

Jesus also celebrated feet. John tells us about tired, worn feet that journeyed with Jesus through Galilee. He washed and tenderly dried feet that had danced with him through the wilderness, feet that had tucked themselves patiently as they sat so often and listened to the words of life. Feet that would run from him the next day, feet that would carry the disciples to the farthest flung corners of the world to announce their love story. These feet were caressed by Jesus with love and with urgency. And he asked them to do the same for each other. If these men and women were to survive the loss they would soon experience, and if they were ever to be able to come to faith in the resurrection, it would be because they removed their shoes and stood on the holy ground of their lives, in their weakness and in their giftedness. When we come together barefoot and exposed, vulnerable and trusting, a new way of loving can happen. Jesus has given us enough grace to journey with him to the cross of Friday. As God freely chose out of love to be bound irrevocably to human mortality, I can also freely choose to accompany Jesus to his passion. I can allow Jesus to make the desperate times of suffering and loss become part of the redemptive work he accomplishes.

Standing together at the cross

A great teacher of mine, Jack Shea, once told me that it wasn't God's will for Jesus to die, just to be. I believe that when Jesus prayed in the garden, it was to remember who he was...the beloved Child of God. And we know that he must have remembered, and the memory sustained him on the cross, so that he could put his life in the hands of Abba. It is not the cross that saves us. The cross itself has no redemptive value, it is the heart of the man on the cross that makes the difference. Suffering does not heal, unless the one who suffers does so for the right reasons and enters into the heart of Christ. As we encounter the crosses in our lives, we have the same struggle to remember who we are, God's beloved children. A great gift of marriage and family is having the company of someone to remind us.

Once when Neil was taking a Scripture course, he had a major paper to write. The week before had been a very traumatic one in our parish, with three young parents dying. As he tried to write, the words wouldn't come, and so he decided to reflect on the losses he had experienced and connect them to the passion of Jesus. He had observed the way our friends had grieved, and noticed that the women expressed their sorrow by holding each other and caring for each other's need. The men had tried to be strong. His final observation moved my heart. He said perhaps the reason the women could find the strength to come to the foot of the cross was that they knew instinctively that they would be held. The men did not have that assurance. His words gave me insight into his need, and showed me clearly the things that men and women have to teach one another. When we can't remember the love, we flee.

There was a time when I did not think I would be able to stand at the foot of the cross I had been given. Someone had hurt our children, and I felt blinding anger and total helplessness. Our deepest sadness was that we had been unable to protect the boys from harm. Working through the feelings, helping the children to heal, and struggling to move toward forgiving was the hardest work I have ever done. One day when the boys were outside playing, I sat at the table and cried. I felt a small arm around my neck, and our son Tom, then nine years old, asked me a question. "Mama, do you still think we can change the world?" I told him I did not, and immediately I regretted it. I said, "But maybe if you and I talk, I can believe again." He said, "Then I have to tell you the truth. I don't know if it can be changed, but it needs to be, so I will try. Will you try?"

It is important to remember that we don't have to carry the cross alone. The love we have shared with others will sustain us when we are crushed under its weight. This past Good Friday we witnessed a stirring enactment of the passion, written by Fr. Bill

Burke and presented by the teens of the parish. The narrators were Luke and the Tempter, who debated at each stop on the journey to Calvary. Luke named the stations for Jesus, and the Tempter tried to plant despair. At each point in the journey Jesus was visited by someone he had healed, someone who had experienced his compassion and love. They told him about the meaning he had given to their lives. Sometimes that is all we need to hear in order to move from death to resurrection.

The hardest part of the paschal mystery, for me, is the waiting of Saturday, when all the demons of self-doubt and fear are running wild. Peter could wait through Saturday, even though he had betrayed Jesus; Judas could not. He could not believe in a God who loves us that much. I am impatient by nature, and I am not all that gracious when I have to wait. I want things now, and usually I want them my way. Often there is a panicky feeling while waiting for test results or for the phone call telling us about a parent who is ill. Sleep is impossible when a child is late, and minutes seem to drag endlessly. In marriage husbands and wives often do not grow at the same time. A difficult and pivotal time in a relationship is the time in between. Neil often finds himself waiting for me to understand a problem. In some areas I am slow to catch on. But his willingness to wait allows me to be able to learn, and I can get to where he is. Other times I am the one out in front. I dream large, and those dreams are occasionally intimidating to Neil. If I belong to him at all, I am called to wait for him to share my dreams. If I push, if I run ahead, we will not share the same dream. Waiting is difficult, yet waiting is an essential part of the journey toward resurrection. It is the time of emptiness that calls forth our deepest surrender to God's love.

A story of resurrection

Surrender in our relationship and with God taught me what I needed to know so that I could wait with my mother and accompany her on her last journey. All of my life my mother and I had had a difficult time. Because she was so ill, both physically and mentally, since I was eleven, there were old, painful memories that were hard to let go of. But several years ago, when her mental illness made it impossible for her to stay in her home, I flew to New York and brought her here to Chicago to a convalescent home four blocks from our house. It was now our turn to care for her, just as my brother and his wife had lived close to our mother and helped care for her for years. I made two promises to myself. The first was that I would simply love her, no strings and no expectations. The second was that I would not allow her to hurt me anymore.

At first her anger made visits hard. I would simply say that I would be back the next day, then I would leave. After a few times she did not strike out, and we enjoyed the quiet of companionship. Neil and I brought her to our home often; I shopped for her and read to her. Our taste in books was vastly different, and I must say I never read so many Danielle Steel books at any other time in my life! For a long time my mother was silent, then slowly she seemed to change. I remember the first time she told me she loved me, then she asked me why I was so good to her. I said it was because she was lovable. Although she did not reply, she thought about it.

One day I received a call from the nurse saying that my mother was dying. We had faced the possibility of her death other times when she had major surgery, or the times when she had tried to take her own life, but this time it was really happening. On my way to the nursing home I prayed that God would give me good memories of my childhood. I was flooded with memories of things from my early years before my mother got sick, things I hadn't thought of in years. I reminded my mother that she once told me about when I was a baby, and she would broil a lamb chop for my dinner and then spend ten minutes scraping the meat with a knife to make a puree. I told her how I thought heating jars in the microwave for our boys was a big deal. She smiled. I told her I remembered the December I could not find my favorite doll, and how on Christmas, under the tree I found "Sweet Sue" nestled in a green trunk filled with dresses, pajamas, and even a pink wool coat with tiny brass buttons, which she had made for me.

Little moments of pleasure, brief glimpses of love, were woven together during those three days she was dying, making a wonderful healing story for her and for me. I asked her forgiveness for any hurts I had given, and I forgave her. For the first time none of those hurts mattered. My brother and his wife flew in from New York, and together we experienced how lovable she really was. I encountered Jesus through my mother's cross, and Easter happened all over again. I will never be the same.

Tell the story

It is essential to recall times when we have met the risen Lord. It is also important to remember that the more we open ourselves to relationship, the more often Jesus will be in our midst. How I understand Easter and how you understand Easter will determine how we will live and worship and grow. During the times of darkness it is helpful to recall and celebrate times in our lives when we experienced resurrection. One thing the disciples did was to tell the stories. It is important for us to tell each other about the times when we worked through pain and distance. The telling brings its own healing and offers hope.

Neil and I have been influenced by the stories of other couples, other people, who have lived their lives in love. When we see the renewal of vows by a couple married for fifty years, we know that fidelity is possible. We know a couple who moved to the inner city to work in a shelter, and we witness the power of self-sacrifice. We have close friends who struggle with the husband's chronic illness, and we are challenged and nourished by their surrender and compassion. Neighbors of ours have adopted several children from different backgrounds, and we see that love has no boundaries. Our parish has a strong Christian Family Movement with over one hundred families, and so our children have grown up in a community that emphasizes family life. In a culture that places individual pleasure first, our children have had an example of community life that challenges misplaced values. In a culture of death these people witness to the power of resurrection.

I really believe that values are caught, not taught. If we settle for relationships marked by alienation and separateness, we will not know the joy of living for each other, and our children will not witness intimacy. But, if we choose, struggle, try to live as one, all our efforts will bear great fruit. I have asked myself, "Why enter the mystery at all?" The only answer that makes sense is the same reason Jesus entered the mystery...to transform the world. When we allow ourselves to be transformed, Easter comes again.

Reflection questions

1. Each stage of life together marks the end of one chapter and the beginning of another. How have you seen the paschal mystery of Jesus in the stages of your life together?

2. When has Easter broken into your darkness?

3. What is the holy ground of your life together? How do you

remove your shoes to stand there?

4. What is the truth that relationship has taught you?

5. Which day of the paschal mystery are you living now? Good Friday? Holy Saturday? Easter Sunday?

6. What gives you the strength to enter the mystery?

Resources

Family the Forming Center, Marjorie Thompson. Nashville: Upper Room.

Marriage and Sacrament: Theology of Christian Marriage, Michael Lawler. Collegeville: Michael Glazier.

Why Marriages Succeed or Fail, John Gottman. New York: Simon and Schuster.

First Two Years of Marriage, Kathleen and Thomas Hart. Mahwah, N.J.: Paulist Press.

Sacred Threshold, Gertrude Mueller Nelson. New York: Image.

Shelter of Each Other, Mary Pipher. New York: Ballantine.

Good Marriage, Wallerstein and Blakeslee. New York: Warner.

Sacred Dwelling, Wendy Wright. New York: Crossroad.

Seasons of a Marriage, H. Norman Wright. Ventura, CA: Regal.

Getting the Love You Want, Harville Hendrix. New York: Harper Perennial.

Marrying Well, James and Evelyn Whitehead. New York: Image.

Family Centered Church, Gerald Foley. Kansas City: Sheed and Ward.

The Theology of the Body, John Paul II. Boston: Pauline Books and Media.

The Role of the Christian Family in the Modern World, John Paul II. Boston: Pauline Books and Media.

Of Related Interest

On Life and Love
A Guide to Catholic Teaching on Marriage and Family
William Urbine & William Seifert
Provides an outline and historical survey of critical documents addressing marriage and family issues from Leo XIII through John Paul II.
0-89622-705-7, 216 pp, $14.95 (B-70)

We Celebrate Our Marriage
John & Laurie Van Bemmel
Stories of married life help spouses share their love and devotion. Makes a thoughtful gift.
0-89622-304-3, 32 pp, $1.95 (BGH)

Marriage Enrichment Series by Brennan & Marie Hill

Communication in Marriage
First in the Marriage Enrichment series, this booklet helps couples to recognize and determine healthy and holy responses to their differences. Great for groups or individual couples.
0-89622- 728-6, 16 pp, $1.95 (M-97)

Intimacy in Marriage
This booklet helps couples focus on love and marriage, share faith and values, and find time to be alone together.
0-89622-744-8, 16 pp, $1.95 (B-50)

Challenges in Marriage
This third booklet looks at family trees and in-laws; acceptance, freeing your partner, and managing money; the challenges of parenting; life changes and passages, and surviving tough times.
0-89622-909-2, 16 pp, $1.95 (B-98)

Bulk prices available. Free Leader's Guide with orders of 10 copies or more.

Available at religious bookstores or from:
TWENTY-THIRD PUBLICATIONS
A Division of Bayard PO BOX 180 • MYSTIC, CT 06355
1-800-321-0411 • FAX: 1-800-572-0788 • E-MAIL: ttpubs@aol.com
www.twentythirdpublications.com
Call for a free catalog